W9-AQK-900

A NEW LIFE OF CHARLOTTE BRONTË

A New Life of Charlotte Brontë

TOM WINNIFRITH

Senior Lecturer in English and Comparative Literary Studies
University of Warwick

St. Martin's Press   New York

First published in the United States of America in 1988

Printed in Hong Kong

ISBN 0–312–01578–X

Library of Congress Cataloging-in-Publication Data
A new life of Charlotte Brontë / Tom Winnifrith.
p.   cm.
Bibliography: p.
includes index.
ISBN 0–312–01578–X: / £30.00 (est.)
1. Brontë, Charlotte, 1816–1855 Biography. 2. Novelists.
English—19th century—Biography. I. Title.
PR4168.W55 1988
823'.8—dc19   87-24164
[B]   CIP

For Frances

Contents

Acknowledgements

My debt to previous scholars is, I hope, clear in my text. Among libraries which have helped me with Brontë manuscripts I should like to mention the British Library, the Brontë Parsonage Museum, the Henry Huntington Library, the Houghton Library in Harvard University, the Humanities Research Center in the University of Texas, the New York Public Library, the Pierpoint Morgan Library and Princeton University Library. For a travel grant to visit American libraries I have to thank the British Academy. I am very grateful to Miss Frances Arnold of Macmillan for her patience and to Miss Debora Stroud for typing the manuscript.

List of Abbreviations

BB	Tom Winnifrith, *The Brontës and their Background* (London, 1973)
BCH	The Bonnell Collection, Haworth
BCL	The Brotherton Collection, Leeds University Library
BCNY	The Berg Collection, New York Public Library
BL	The British Library
BPM	The Brontë Parsonage Museum, Haworth
BST	*Brontë Society Transactions*
CW	Edward Chitham and Tom Winnifrith, *Brontë Facts and Brontë Problems* (London, 1983)
FWM	The Fitzwilliam Museum, Cambridge
G	E. C. Gaskell, *The Life of Charlotte Brontë*, Haworth Edition (London, 1899)
HLC	The Henry Huntington Library, California
HRT	The Humanities Research Centre, University of Texas
HUL	The Houghton Library, Harvard University
PML	The Pierpoint Morgan Library, New York
PUL	The Princeton University Library
SHBP	*The Poems of Patrick Branwell Brontë*, edited by Tom Winnifrith (London, 1983)
SHCP	*The Poems of Charlotte Brontë*, edited by Tom Winnifrith (London, 1984)
SHLL	*The Brontës: Their Lives, Friendships and Correspondence*, edited by T. J. Wise and J. S. Symington, 4 vols (London, 1932)

Introduction

Writing a new life of Charlotte Brontë is rather like going for a walk on the moors above Haworth. There are familiar landmarks and unexpected views, both of great beauty. There are dreary stretches, hidden pitfalls and sudden squalls which blow up out of nowhere. The twisting paths and the complexities of Charlotte's life have been well covered, but seem still to be insufficiently appreciated. There is a timeless quality about the landscape and about Charlotte's story, but against this one has to balance grim relics from the nineteenth century and garish intrusions from the twentieth.

There is no lack of fellow wanderers on the moors and no shortage of other writers about the Brontës. It is discourteous to condemn the efforts of one's predecessors. Mrs Gaskell's *Life of Charlotte Brontë* is a monument to biography, to Victorian good taste and to her friendship with her fellow author. With Charlotte's father and husband breathing down her neck, with Charlotte's best friend supplying letters in a niggardly and prudish fashion, with the scandal at Cowan Bridge to the left of her, with the scandal of Branwell to the right of her, and the greater scandal of Monsieur Heger in front of her – to be firmly left behind under close wraps – it was a miracle that Mrs Gaskell produced anything at all. As it was she produced a Victorian classic, admired at the time, and admired even now, more perhaps than her own novels. It is true that the scandals to the left and right caught up with her fairly soon, and resulted in a bowdlerised third edition, and that inevitably the scandal from behind came to the forefront of Brontë studies after the discovery of Charlotte's letters to Monsieur Heger in 1914. Nevertheless it is still true that no student of Charlotte Brontë can study her without the help of Mrs Gaskell, just as it is unfortunately true that no student of the Brontës, eager for objective truth and relying on modern scholarly methods, can rely on Mrs Gaskell's account which, for the best of reasons, is partial in more than one sense.

Mrs Gaskell has had many successors; the attraction of her book inspired inferior imitators. The discovery of the Heger letters suggested that, if biographical gold mines lay beneath the cobblestones of Brussels, they could be found elsewhere. No other English author has forged such a close link between the place where he or she wrote and the places about which they wrote. Shakespeare scholars have not investigated gentlemen in Verona, but Brontë students have combed Yorkshire and Brussels for clues about the Brontës. All too often their findings have been ludicrously unscholarly. Students of Emily Brontë, about whom there is far less evidence than there is for Charlotte, may know a book in which an imaginary lover for Emily is suggested, a Belgian, named Louis Parensell.[1] The whole book is built upon a misreading of a title of one of Emily's poems, 'Love's Farewell'. Books about Charlotte, where there is both more irrefutable evidence and more evidence to be refuted, have tended to follow the same pattern, though in a less eccentric fashion.

Among such books there have been two which have bid fair to rival Mrs Gaskell's *Life* in popular esteem. Margaret Lane's *The Brontë Story* (London, 1953) aimed to bring Mrs Gaskell up to date, both by including the other Brontës, as her title indicates, and by introducing new discoveries about the Brontës, especially the evidence of the letters to Monsieur Heger. She is full of invaluable insights into Mrs Gaskell's difficulties. Her accounts of Branwell, Emily and Anne are made more moving by Joan Hassall's imaginative woodcuts. The book is fair to all four Brontës, but relying as it does principally on secondary evidence does not pretend to be a learned or an authoritative account.

Rather different is Winifred Gerin's *Charlotte Brontë: The Evolution of Genius* (Oxford, 1966). This book's length, extensive quotations and impressive format meant that it won scholarly acclaim as well as deservedly attracting popular support for its success in bringing the Brontë legend to life. Miss Gerin, who also skilfully wrote books on the other three Brontë children and on Mrs Gaskell without repeating her material, clearly incorporated a great many facts into her account, and all students of the Brontës are greatly in her debt. It is a pity that on examination many of her facts turn out not to be facts at all, but hypotheses that have been turned into facts in the century since Charlotte Brontë died. These hypotheses are based upon uncertain oral tradition, unreliable manuscripts, an inadequate knowledge of Victorian social and religious history and the habit, almost endemic among writers on the Brontës, of treating their books as if they were autobiographies.

In *The Brontës and their Background* (London, 1973) I pointed out these faults perhaps a little too harshly, possibly not paying sufficient attention to the way in which real events suggested, rather than dictated, events in Charlotte's novels. I did point out that the major stumbling block in the way of a scholarly life of any of the Brontës was the inadequate way in which the primary manuscript evidence had been handled and edited. The position has now been improved. The novels are now being edited properly, although there was never much doubt about the text of the novels. The poems have also received critical attention, and – though it is even more dangerous to make biographical assumptions from poetry than it is from novels – at least we can now be fairly certain when the poems were written, who was the author, and what they said. The juvenilia, about which there has been much speculation, are in the process of being edited, and Dr Christine Alexander has given us a foretaste of their contents in *The Early Writings of Charlotte Brontë* (London, 1983). Only the letters await a satisfactory edition. It is true that letters would seem to form the basis of any biography, and both Mrs Gaskell and Miss Gerin quote extensively from Charlotte's correspondence. Once we are aware of the inaccuracy, omissions and incorrect datings which mar such editions as The Shakespeare Head edition (London, 1932, reprinted 1980) we can, by checking available manuscripts, do something to remedy this deficiency.

It is of course possible that somewhere under the fast-disappearing cobblestones of Brussels, or in some remote Irish rectory, or in some rich American library, a new piece of evidence will turn up to shed new and unexpected light on the Brontë story. The indefatigable Brontë Society has produced many small additions to our knowledge of the Brontës, and has recorded them in the *Brontë Society Transactions*. It is unlikely that any shattering discoveries will now emerge; finds like the Heger letters only occur once in a blue moon.

The time would then seem to be right for a new look at Charlotte Brontë, based on all available evidence, carefully sifted for any inaccuracies. It may be asked why a biography is valuable, and this question is pertinent at a time when various critical theories are fairly dismissive about the importance of an author's life in the study of his or her works. The Brontës have always been at the mercy of critics ready to fit them into their own moral, psychological and political straitjackets. Feminist criticism, often perceptive, sometimes far fetched, is particularly fashionable. This book has no axe to grind, but aims to see Charlotte Brontë and to see her whole. Matthew Arnold, a discriminating student of the Brontës, would approve of this aim, even though its apparent objectivity now tends to be dismissed as yet another partial subjective view.[2] Too many books on the Brontës have a partial and unsteady air.

We want to know about Charlotte Brontë because she is a writer of famous books, and we want to know about her because she is a human being of singular pathos. It is very difficult to draw the line between these two demands. I have tried to meet them both, but not to blur the distinction between them, as I think Miss Gerin and a host of other writers do when they assume that Charlotte was writing her autobiography in her novels.

Charlotte's life was drab and uneventful. The loss of her mother at an early age, her unhappiness at school, both as pupil and as teacher, her lack of success as a governess, her unrequited love for Monsieur Heger, the disgrace of Branwell, followed by his death and that of Emily and Anne, the loneliness of early middle age, terminated by the tepid courtship with Mr Nicholls, the brief period of marriage, and then Charlotte's own death may seem tragic, but they are not really exciting, nor particularly unusual at a time when life expectancy and expectations in life were considerably less than is the case at the present time. What makes them exciting and unusual is that the person who experienced them was able both to translate and transcend them and become a great novelist. This fact, of course, heightens the pathos of the life; it is especially poignant that Charlotte was at her most unhappy in the early 1850s when, as the author of two successful novels, she could look forward to fame, wealth and security, but for a period of six months was unable to find anyone with whom she could exchange anything but the most basic conversation.[3]

Charlotte as an authoress makes Charlotte the woman interesting, but Charlotte Brontë is not Jane Eyre, Frances Henri, Caroline Helstone or Lucy Snowe any more than Monsieur Heger is Paul Emanuel, Henry Nussey is St John Rivers or George Smith is John Graham Bretton; the list of identifications both for persons and places is almost as endless as it is useless. On the other hand Charlotte Brontë was the creator of her heroines, and her heroes have, as school masters or Belgians or married men, some points in common with a certain married Belgian schoolmaster. It is because she was an authoress that the events of Charlotte Bronte's life are interesting to us, but we must not forget that the events of her life are sources of inspiration to the authoress.

I have tried to keep these considerations in mind when writing this new life, emphasising those parts of Charlotte's life which have most bearing on her career as an author. Mr Nicholls, for example, does not play much of a part in the following account: Charlotte wrote but little after she had married him. It is interesting but profitless to speculate what Charlotte might have been allowed to write if she had lived. The juvenilia, although they are beginning to be unravelled thanks to the labours of Dr Alexander, do not figure as prominently as in some recent accounts. They are testimony to Charlotte's apprenticeship as a writer, but not as a good writer. Charlotte's father, brother and two sisters have clearly an important role in Charlotte's story, but I am writing the life of Charlotte Brontë and not a general account of the Brontës. The fact that Charlotte was in her lifetime the most famous of the three sisters, the fact that Ellen Nussey kept her letters, and the fact that Charlotte was the Brontë who in her novels remained closest to her experiences makes the writing of her life easier and more profitable than that of any of her kindred.

The Charlotte that emerges from the following pages is an admirable but not a particularly attractive figure. The tendency to turn biography into hagiography must be resisted. Mrs Gaskell, in spite of the formidable difficulties in her way, was quite good at presenting the oddness, the bitterness, the loneliness and the unhappiness that marred Charlotte's life. Ellen Nussey, who had supplied Mrs Gaskell with much of her material, was angry that a more dutiful and orthodox portrait did not emerge, although Ellen's hostility to Mr Brontë and Mr Nicholls must have made it hard for anyone to see Charlotte as a dutiful wife and daughter through her eyes.[4] Yesterday's heterodoxy is today's orthodoxy. The biography of Tennyson by Hallam Tennyson is a remarkable piece of Victorian reticence, but makes the poet out to be dull and stodgy. This is not the impression we form after the discoveries of Sir Charles Tennyson who has made the wild, unhappy and more than slightly mad poet infinitely preferable to modern sensibilities.[5] Without any descendants the Brontës have been more at the mercy of popular whims, and recent biographers and critics have tended to see the sisters as pioneer feminists and revolutionaries, although this attitude is hotly resented by their Yorkshire admirers anxious to protect the memory of their patron saints.

The truth lies probably between these two extremes. It may be a disadvantage to be neither from Yorkshire nor a woman when it comes to writing about the Brontës especially since some of the most famous Brontë biographers have been both. But a detached observer

need not be as purblind as Emily Brontë's Lockwood, and can avoid
some of the difficulties of close involvement faced by Nelly Dean. As
a writer Charlotte produced two very different masterpieces in *Jane
Eyre* and *Villette*. Would we read *Shirley* and *The Professor* without
these two greater books in mind? Some of Charlotte's poetry and
some of her juvenilia are interesting, and in a few pieces we can see
traces of genius. But most of the juvenilia is sad stuff, incoherent
and rambling, never being intended for publication. The stories and
poems do have a certain relevance for the biographer, but not really
for students of literature.

Nor must the biographer be blind to certain faults in Charlotte's
character. Her failures as a governess and teacher were largely her
own fault. She did not like children and resented her subordinate
position. She had difficulty in making friends, although she did
retain the loyalty of two very different schoolfellows, Ellen Nussey
and Mary Taylor. It is a great pity that the original and courageous
Mary Taylor did not preserve her correspondence. The letters to
Ellen Nussey are occasionally patronising and sometimes narrow
and spiteful, but perhaps Ellen deserved the former response and
contributed to the latter.

To her immediate family Charlotte's attitude was not perfect. Few
can doubt her devotion to her sisters, although relations cannot
have always been easy in their lifetime, and after their death
Charlotte does not seem to have been very sensitive to their work.
Mr Nicholls and Mr Brontë were, like Charlotte, difficult and lonely
individuals, without her redeeming genius. Ellen Nussey may have
been right in thinking they did not deserve her, although some
might see Charlotte's loyalty to her father and husband as a rather
touching weakness. Charlotte's feelings towards Monsieur Heger
would, if known, have caused a Victorian scandal; to modern
students they cause mild surprise that she did not translate these
feelings into action. Here, as in the similar case with Branwell, it is
important that we avoid both nineteenth-century prudery and
twentieth-century prurience in order to discover, if it is at all
possible, exactly what happened before passing judgement.

Like many of us, Charlotte Brontë was muddled by the conflicting
claims of reason and emotion, duty and inclination, religion and
passion. Unlike most of us she was – in her books, if not in her life –
capable of resolving these conflicts. This book explores both the
conflicts and the resolution. Matthew Arnold, previously held up
for admiration, described *Villette* as full of hunger, rebellion and

rage. Later he relented in 'Haworth Church Yard', perhaps in this poem yielding too much to the tendency to equate biography with hagiography. Charlotte Brontë was both admirable and pitiable; we should not be condescending to her books or be rhapsodic about the trivial details of her life.

1
Origins

Charlotte begins her last novel by talking of the Brettons of Bretton, figures of established position and sources of solid British comfort, to whom the friendless Lucy Snowe turns at moments of crisis, but to whose secure position she realises eventually that she cannot aspire. The Brontës were not Brontës of Brontë. Brontë is in fact the name of a place in Sicily which Lord Nelson took as part of his title when ennobled, and it was no doubt the connection with Lord Nelson, an obvious hero in the Brontë family, that led Charlotte's father to adopt this name in place of the more humble Prunty under which he was born.

It is perhaps fanciful to read too much into this simple change of name, quite common at a time when spelling had hardly been regularised. Even if the change to Brontë does suggest a certain snobbery on Mr Brontë's part, this snobbery seems relatively harmless, and it is not immediately clear to what extent the adoption of the new aristocratic-sounding name is a conscious effort to throw off an obscure and slightly disreputable Irish ancestry. Unfortunately the whole subject of this Irish ancestry is a vexed one, although thanks to the efforts of Dr Edward Chitham many of the obscurities have now been unravelled.[1]

It is known for certain that Mr Brontë was born in a poor household in Ireland, and that by his efforts, his learning and his piety he succeeded in entering Cambridge and the Church, thus leaping at one bound a great class barrier in an age when such barriers were much more difficult to leap. Difficult, but not impossible if one had good friends, worked hard and entered the Church. My own great-grandfather, the illegitimate son of a blacksmith, ended his life as a rector of Hythe, a prosperous town in Kent, although Jude the Obscure was a little less lucky.

American readers of the Brontës, used to the transition from log cabin to White House, and modern readers, to whom the whole subject of social class and social snobbery is distasteful, may find the subject of Mr Brontë's social origins boring and irrelevant to a consideration of the life of Charlotte Brontë. But even the most liberated of us must owe something to our parents in forming our views, even if they only act as a source of outmoded doctrines against which we can rebel. Charlotte, though rebellious in other ways, never seems to have rebelled consciously against her father, and Mr Brontë, whatever his faults, seems to have been a strong character. He certainly needed his strength to withstand the disasters that befell him in later life, and to enjoy the opportunities that befell him in his extraordinary early life. As what is now rather coyly called a single parent, Mr Brontë suffered many disadvantages, but such parents can usually count on their children's affection and respect.

Mr Brontë, although at times apparently detached and withdrawn, appears to have commanded considerable respect from his children. Thus, even if we knew nothing of his early life, we could perhaps guess at his views and their origin from the attitudes of his daughters. A strong hostility to Catholicism and to the Irish in Charlotte's novels and juvenilia may make the Irish Catholic origins of Mr Brontë's family surprising, but a convert is always eager to disassociate himself from his former faith. The enthusiasm of the Brontë children for literature and learning, though touching and at times misplaced, is not surprising, since it was through this route that Mr Brontë had raised himself. Above all in their distaste for, ignorance of, but secret hankering after an aristocratic world the Brontës may be reflecting the uprooting of their father from his odd Irish background, itself perhaps with vaguely aristocratic affiliations, to an alien environment where Mr Brontë's education and profession cut him off from those below him, while his origins and his character cut him off from those above.

The Brontës had of course a mother as well as a father. Themselves keenly interested in how far nurture and and how far nature is responsible for the character of children, the Brontës would demand that Maria Branwell and her family are discussed in this chapter, even though admitting that it was the loss of their mother which influenced the children more than any genes she may have passed on to them. Maria Branwell was obviously very different from Patrick Brontë, and yet the marriage was a happy one as well as being one for which generations of English literature students have every reason to be happy. In spite of their differences in character Mr and Mrs Brontë shared a Celtic origin and a Low Church religion. Racial theories, though quite all right for high-minded liberals like Matthew Arnold, and Mrs Humphry Ward,[2] are now unfashionable and rightly so, and yet it is impossible to dismiss entirely the belief that the Brontës owed their sad, sorrowing gift for words to their Celtic ancestry. Religious distinctions are likewise out of fashion, and again perhaps this is right, although again we can admire the fierce Evangelical zeal for truth and high standards of moral conduct which united both adult Brontës with their daughters.

The Reverend Patrick Brontë was born on St Patrick's Day, 17 March 1777. Amid a plethora of easily forgettable legends about the Irish Brontës this date seems comfortingly memorable and certain, although we only have Mrs Gaskell's word for it. No record survives of Patrick's birth or baptism, but Mrs Gaskell presumably derived her information from the old man himself, and one does not forget one's birthday. Patrick was succeeded into the world by four brothers and then, in a fairly unlikely combination, by five sisters. Of the brothers William fought in the rebellion of 1798, Hugh and James did not marry, and are supposed to have visited Haworth, while Welsh is alleged to have been more gentlemanly than the other brothers. Not much is known of the five sisters. Jane died young, Mary is the recipient of one of Mr Brontë's letters, Sarah – whom Charlotte rather pathetically said she wished she knew – married Simon Collins, but almost nothing is heard of her twin Rose, while the youngest sister Alice, born in 1796, survived until 1891. This generation of Brontës, unlike the famous next generation was, with the exception of Jane, remarkable for their longevity. Only four out of ten children married. There may have been many reasons for this and rural poverty was probably one of them. It is also possible that, like their famous nieces, this generation was both in character and situation rather different from their neighbours.

Patrick Brontë left Ireland in 1802. There were infrequent visits from him to Ireland, and from his Irish kindred to England. These are difficult to date or to substantiate, and we are not helped by colourful and improbable legends to the effect that Patrick's brother Hugh came over to England armed with a shillelagh to belabour the unkind reviewer of *Jane Eyre* in *The Quarterly Review*. Patrick claimed to have sent money back to his family, and to have left them money in his will, although the exact extent of his generosity cannot be determined. Before the establishment of the postal service, communication between Yorkshire and Ireland must have been difficult and indeed before 1840 we only have evidence of one letter from Patrick to Ireland in 1812, although others were certainly written. In the last years. of his life Patrick seems to have had fairly regular contact with his family. They were perhaps proud of their famous connection, and he, deprived of his daughters, must have been lonely.

We do not of course have the correspondence of Patrick Brontë in anything like as complete a fashion as we have the letters of Charlotte, and it is the absence of any mention of Ireland by Charlotte in her letters, as well as her hostility to Ireland in her books, which suggests that Mr Brontë was not particularly dutiful in keeping close links with Ireland. Before condemning him too harshly we must remember how difficult it must have been to maintain links. Travel to and from Ireland cannot have been particularly easy or cheap. Like Mr Earnshaw in *Wuthering Heights*, anyone travelling between Yorkshire and Liverpool may well have had to go on foot. Even in the age of the telephone and the aeroplane we know how easy it is to lose contact with friends and family, and how hard it is to renew a friendship after an embarrassing break in communication.

Mr Brontë had come from a humble home, and was naturally not terribly proud of this. But as well as poverty, the peculiarity of the Brontë lineage may have caused embarrassment, although it seems likely that Mr Brontë was not reluctant to entertain his children with tales from this extraordinary past. It is difficult to detach fact from legend. It is not only the Irish who tell tall stories, although they have a particular reputation for doing so. The Reverend William Wright heard many anecdotes about Mr Brontë's Irish ancestors, some of which bore similarities with the plots of the Brontë novels. He may have been led astray. Yorkshire patriotism dismissed William Wright as credulous, although some of those attacking him such as Clement Shorter and Horsfall Turner do not have a very good reputation as disinterested scholars. It is true that Mr Brontë amused his children with tales from Yorkshire as well as from Ireland, and both elements entered the novels of the three Brontë sisters as well as the third precious element of the shaping imagination. It is as fruitless to look for the key to *Wuthering Heights* and *Jane Eyre* in the Mountains of Mourne as it is on the moors of Haworth. Nevertheless the story of Mr Brontë's father is probably much as Wright told it, and does much to explain the Brontës' isolation.

Mrs Gaskell says vaguely that Mr Brontë's father, Hugh Prunty, had come from the south of Ireland to the north, and that there was a dim tradition of some noble ancestry. This would seem to be based on a letter from Patrick himself. The researches of Wright and Chitham have shown that it is likely that Hugh Prunty was brought up by a cruel uncle called Welsh near the River Boyne. This is not very far south from the place where Patrick was born, although it is now in the Irish Republic as opposed to Northern Ireland. Tragically the border is far more important in 1985 than in 1855 or 1777, but there was always something of a division between County Down and the country near Dundalk, sufficient to give some meaning to the vague statement about Patrick coming from the south of Ireland.

So Mr Brontë is not all that wrong about the south. The noble ancestry may be harder to swallow, although not if we also believe Wright's account of how Hugh Prunty was taken on a long journey by his Uncle Welsh. This journey has been calculated by Dr Edward Chitham as being probably one from south west Ulster, Tyrone, Monaghan or Cavan where the name Prunty, O'Prunty or Prontaigh is common. There is even an Irish poet, Padraigh O'Pronantaigh, who may have been related to Hugh Prunty.[3]

Welsh Prunty's cruel treatment of the young Hugh has a certain amount in common with the story of Heathcliff, and there are long journeys, lonely children and harsh relatives in a number of Brontë novels, notably *Jane Eyre*. More importantly the Irish ancestry of the Brontës, if it could be proved, would do much to explain their gift for story-telling, their social isolation and in a strange way their religion.

It is almost certain that Hugh Prunty was a Catholic, probable that he was Irish speaking, and possible that he was closely related to those practised in the oral bardic tradition. The young Brontës seem to have acquired the gift of composing almost spontaneously both in verse and prose. There is no evidence for Mr Brontë encouraging these activities, but no evidence for him discouraging them either. Talents can be inherited rather than handed down, and we should probably reckon the sagas of Gondal and Angria, loosely constructed rather like oral epics, with the same high note of heroism and despair, to be an unconscious rather than a conscious reflection by the Brontës of their Irish heritage.

In Charlotte's novels the Irish are despised, but Catholicism is actively disliked. This may be due to her experiences in Belgium, but there is evidence of hostility to Catholicism in the juvenilia. In Ireland Mr Brontë and his family must have endured a certain amount of disapproval as the children of Catholics, and this may explain why so few of them married. In England he never appears to have given any hints of his Catholic ancestry, and his Evangelical religion and Tory politics would seem to have cast him into the opposite camp. Catholics were never popular in the nineteenth century, especially during such flashpoints as the Catholic Relief Act of 1829 or the defection of Newman to Rome in 1845. Mr Brontë's dislike of Mr Nicholls may be due to the latter's High Church leanings as well as to his Irish origin, although the more human motives of paternal jealousy and the feeling that his daughter deserved someone more distinguished must not be discounted.

Odi et amo. Behind the Brontë's dislike of Catholicism lies a curious fascination with it. Charlotte's well-known visit to the confessional and her love for Monsieur Heger reflect this ambivalence. Mr Brontë seemed to have no objection to his two daughters going off to Catholic Belgium, and spent a little time there himself. Charlotte more than once, admittedly with disapproval, links the extreme Low Church with the extreme High Church. It was a curious phenomenon of the Oxford Movement of the 1840s that so many of its most famous disciples were sons of leaders of the Evangelical Movement at the beginning of the century.[4]

Mr Brontë's own religion was closely connected with his schooling. At the age of sixteen we find him teaching at Glascar, a Presbyterian meeting house, Like his daughters subsequently, and like many another character in nineteenth-century fiction, Patrick appears to have passed from being pupil to teacher almost without effort, the dividing line being fairly flexible. The temporary allegiance to Presbyterianism may seem odd in view of Patrick's Catholic past and his Anglican future, but the Presbyterians were on the same side as the Catholics in Wolf Tone's rebellion of 1798, and their Low Church faith was not dissimilar to Evangelical Anglicanism. Patrick, unlike his daughters, seems to have been a successful teacher, but in about 1798 gave up his post at Glascar. A scandalous story that he had become too friendly with one of his female pupils may be true, and may have been the reason for his dismissal. This cannot have been an easy year in Ireland, and Patrick's brother William had joined the rebels.

By about 1800 Patrick had become friendly with the Reverend Thomas Tighe, the Anglican but Evangelical minister of Drumballyroney. His motives for the change of allegiance and his exact position in the Tighe household are both obscure. He claimed in a letter to Mrs Gaskell that he was tutor to a gentleman's sons, but

Tighe's descendants have denied this. It is more probable that like his daughters after him, he was both pupil to Mr Tighe and teacher to village children as at Glascar. Mr Tighe, a friend of Wesley, was almost certainly the spur to Patrick leaving Ireland for Cambridge, where he matriculated as Patrick Brontë in October 1802. He had saved seven pounds, and was given five pounds, but was only able to survive at Cambridge by being a sizar, someone who performed menial duties for the richer undergraduates. There is speculation in *Wuthering Heights* that Heathcliff may have risen to being a gentleman by the same route.

Being a sizar cannot have been an easy or congenial task, but Mr Brontë's character, his age (at twenty-five he was much older than the average student), his piety and his learning carried him through. Some of the classical texts which he won as college prizes still survive, and he remained a reasonable classical scholar throughout his life. In 1804 we find two famous names in the Evangelical Movement, Henry Martyn and William Wilberforce, corresponding about Mr Brontë, whom they see as an instrument of good to the Church. With the renewal of hostilities against Napoleon, Mr Brontë took part in the college army corps, boasting in later life that the future Lord Palmerston had served with him. An interest in warfare was something that he passed on to his children. It seems odd that war and religion should go together, as Charlotte saw when she said of Mr Helstone in *Shirley* that he should have been a soldier rather than a priest, but Mr Helstone is not modelled on Mr Brontë, and war was more chivalrous in those days, although hatred of Napoleon was more intense than any similar hatred now.

Mr Brontë graduated in 1806 at the age of twenty-nine, and after a brief visit home, when he preached at Drumballyroney, he took up his duties at Wethersfield in Essex as a curate in an Evangelical parish. In 1807 he was ordained priest, but a love-affair with a certain Mary Burder came to grief, probably because of the obscurity of Mr Brontë's origins, as his prospects must have been good. Both in *Agnes Grey* and *Jane Eyre* the heroine's mother is disowned for marrying a poor clergyman, and the theme of marriage between a woman of superior and a man of inferior rank occurs in almost all the Brontë novels. There was nothing particularly superior about Mary Burder, and Mr Brontë is hardly likely to have talked much about her to his children especially after the tragi-comedy of a second rejection when the recently widowed Mr Brontë wrote pathetically to his former love and was devastatingly snubbed. Nevertheless his hurt pride in this instance may have been passed on unconsciously to his daughters.

In 1809 Mr Brontë moved briefly to Wellington in Shropshire, but in the same year, helped by Mrs Fletcher, widow of Wesley's successor, was appointed to a curacy at Dewsbury in Yorkshire. The move to Yorkshire, though fortunate, was also not entirely for- tuitous, as Yorkshire was a stronghold of Methodism and Evangeli- calism, the simplicity of the Low Church message being a better solace for those working in the harsh conditions of that area than more conventional and insincere pieties. We hear stories of Mr Brontë's rather eccentric courage at Dewsbury, and it is in this area and at this time that Charlotte sets her novel *Shirley*.

Two prominent conflicts in *Shirley* are those between the Luddite handloom weavers and the mill-owners trying to introduce machin- ery, and between the Nonconformists and members of the Church of England. In both cases Charlotte may be influenced by her own times, linking the Chartists with the Luddites, and exaggerating the rivalry between the Anglicans and Nonconformists. John Wesley remained a clergyman of the Church of England all his life, and Mr Brontë, in going to Haworth, was taking up a post previously occupied by William Grimshaw, who had been third in the Evangelical hierarchy after Wesley and Whitfield. The distinction between Wesleyans and Evangelicals was a very hard one to draw in the years before Mr Brontë's marriage and makes his marriage to Maria Branwell less surprising. At Wellington, Patrick Brontë's fellow curate had been a William Morgan. William Morgan, of whom Charlotte was later to speak not very kindly, moved to Bradford and became engaged to Jane, daughter of John Fennell, the headmaster of a Wesleyan School at Woodhouse Grove. Mr Brontë, who had moved to Hartshead from Dewsbury in 1811, was invited to the school as an examiner in 1812, and there met and fell in love with Jane's cousin, Maria Branwell, the daughter of Thomas Branwell and Anne Carne. The Branwells were a prominent Methodist family in Cornwall, another area where Wesley had attracted many converts. Maria's brother, Benjamin, had already been Mayor of Penzance.

Neither Maria nor Patrick was in their first youth, Maria being born in 1783, but it seems to have been a genuine love-match on both sides. Maria's surviving letters show this clearly. Nor with the obvious approval of John Fennell and the parallel engagement of William Morgan and Jane Fennell could there have been any question of the Branwell family objecting to the match. There was a double wedding on 29 December 1812 with Patrick and William taking it in turns to be clergyman and bridegroom.

Little is known about Maria Brontë who vanishes so swiftly and sadly from the Brontë story. Her letters are well written, full of sincerity and good sense. The Branwells appear to have been unremarkable but respectable people who perhaps added a strain of common sense to Mr Brontë's rather wayward genius. There was a large family, but with the important exception of Elizabeth Branwell, Maria's elder sister, no very close links between the Branwells in Cornwall and the Yorkshire Brontës seem to have been kept up, distance being probably the reason. We hear of one visit by some 'August' relations from London who stayed with Uncle Fennell in 1840; 'August' may be an allusion to the month, but Charlotte does not speak very kindly of these particular relations.[5] In 1851 Charlotte and Mr Brontë received an unexpected call from a cousin in Cornwall. There is no reason apart from Charlotte's harsh remark about Uncle Fennell being well-rid of his guests to suspect that there was any ill feeling between the two families.

Both Maria's parents were dead by the time she met her husband, and she brought with her a small but respectable annuity of £50. Their first two children, Maria and Elizabeth, were both born while Mr Brontë was the incumbent at Hartshead, but on 19 May 1815 he exchanged livings with the Reverend Thomas Atkinson of Thornton, and it was at Thornton, five miles to the west of Haworth that the remaining children were born, Charlotte on 21 April 1816, Patrick on 26 June 1817, Emily on 30 July 1818 and Anne on 17 January 1820. The strain of these constant births in a small house must have been considerable, although Miss Branwell, as if foreshadowing the future, did make numerous visits.

During these years Mr Brontë produced a number of works in prose and verse. Neither the stories nor the poetry have any literary merit, although they are characterised by a strong moralistic strain.[6] Nevertheless Mr Brontë cannot be written off completely when we are looking for literary influences on his daughters. What role Mr Brontë played in bringing up his daughters is hard to determine. We do get a slight glimpse of life at Thornton from the diary of Miss Elizabeth Firth, the daughter of the grandest inhabitant of Thornton, John Firth of Kipping House.[7] Relations between the two families were friendly, and a prodigious amount of tea was drunk.

Miss Firth was godmother to Elizabeth and to Anne. There is a tradition that Mr Brontë proposed marriage to Miss Firth after his wife's death, but she married another clergyman, a Mr Franks. The Firths were quite rich with smart relations, the Walkers, who lived at Lascelles Hall, one of whom married Mr Atkinson, Mr Brontë's predecessor at Thornton. Charlotte in her later letters speaks ill of these Walkers,[8] and it is just possible that the patronising nature of the relationship between the Firths and the Brontës angered her. We know that Mr and Mrs Franks visited the Brontës at Cowan Bridge; we hear of one visit to Lowood by the smartly dressed Brocklehurst family.

This association may be conjecture and the general impression we form from Miss Firth's diary is of a friendly, happy, sociable atmosphere with Mr Brontë, far from being patronised, a great comfort to Mr Firth at the time of his death. Stories of Mr Brontë's eccentricity as a husband and father derive from Mrs Gaskell's life, and have generally been discounted. Whether or not Mr Brontë burnt boots, cut up his wife's dress and stuffed the hearthrug up the chimmney is now hard to ascertain.[9] It looks as if for reasons of temperament as well as convention Mr Brontë was the dominant partner of the marriage. This was of course the convention of the day, and Mr Brontë's age and profession must have helped his authority.

It has been remarked that the Brontës who drew so freely on their experiences for their books have as their heroines characters who are bereft not of one but of two parents. Agnes Grey has a mother, Caroline Helstone finds her mother halfway through the book, and, although both Mr Earnshaw and Edgar Linton die early, there are some observations on fatherly love in *Wuthering Heights*. Charlotte's two most famous heroines are entirely on their own throughout *Jane Eyre* and *Villette*, and this fact makes the books more interesting. It is, however, unlikely that the young Brontës felt themselves bereft of a father as well as a mother. There is nothing in Charlotte's correspondence to betray any lack of affection and respect for her father, and this is true in spite of the fact that most of her letters were to Ellen Nussey who disliked Mr Brontë. Both God and Mammon dictated that Mr Brontë was estremely important in his children's eyes, since with his death they would lose their home and be cast out into the world, as Jane Eyre and Lucy Snowe are. The relationship between parent and child is an extremely difficult and delicate one, especially if there is only one parent, and the Brontës would seem to have got round this difficulty by not describing many parents in their works.

From Mrs Gaskell onwards biographers have tended to paint Mr Brontë in an exaggerated light. He is generally seen as a typical Victorian paterfamilias, overbearing, selfish and tyrannical, with a streak of eccentric unreliability in addition, responsible for his daughters' sorrow, and unappreciative of their virtues. Alternatively he emerges as a heroic figure singlehandedly coping with the demands of his profession and his difficult children under a series of blows, any one of which would have reduced a weaker man to drink or despair. The truth, as the following pages will illustrate, lies somewhere between these two extremes.

2

Pupil

The Brontës are so inextricably linked with Haworth that it is sometimes forgotten that none of them were born there, or that none of their books are set in a village like Haworth. The successive moves of Mr Brontë had taken him steadily westward, but there is nothing further west of Haworth except stretches of barren moorland until one comes to Lancashire. His position as perpetual curate of Haworth brought his in a steady if not substantial income, and the post was an important one as the parish was large, and Grimshaw had made the church famous. Personal circumstances would have probably prevented Mr Brontë from moving if he had wished to, but there is no indication that he ever contemplated such a step, or that any form of promotion was offered to him.

Haworth was rather different from other positions that Mr Brontë had held. The inhabitants were stubbornly independent, and had made difficulties for the previous incumbent. There were obstacles to Mr Brontë himself being appointed. Mrs Gaskell, no stranger to the harsh life of the north in her life or in her books, commented on the rough savagery of the inhabitants. Charlotte herself commented in a letter of 1840 that a lecture by her father and Mr Weightman was considered remarkable in the local newspaper as emanating from Haworth, 'situated among the bogs and mountains and until very lately supposed to be in a state of semi-barbarism'.[1]

Even today with the refinements of modern civilisation and the tawdry trappings of tourism Haworth has a peculiar air about it. The church has been replaced by a more modern building, most of the upright tombstones in the sombre churchyard are later than the Brontës, the Parsonage has been altered and the moors have been encroached upon. But the steep main street remains much as it did on the day when a cart rumbled slowly up with the Brontës' possessions piled high upon it. This day was well remembered by old inhabitants of the village, and many Brontë biographers begin with it.

With the move to Haworth the Brontë story, which had hitherto had an air of humdrum success about it, took on the sadness and

19

loneliness which we have come to associate with the Brontës. In Thornton the Firths had been friendly, and Mr Brontë had had plenty of clergymen to talk to. The remoteness of Haworth made visiting cumbersome. Contact with the humble village people was difficult. The grandest people in the village were the Heatons of Ponden House. More work could be done on contact between these two families, although the Heaton children were not the right age to be friends with the Brontë children who used the Ponden House library. Like the Brontës, the Heatons appear to have been slightly odd, and this shared characteristic cannot have made friendship any easier, although Emily seems to have derived much of the inspiration for *Wuthering Heights* from her contact with the Heatons, whose name may be the inspiration for both Hareton and Heathcliff.[2]

Had Mrs Brontë lived she might have found friends for her family, but weakened by the birth of six children in six years, she became ill at the end of January 1821, and died seven months later. The illness, a form of cancer, was a distressing one and Mr Brontë, in a painful letter to Miss Burder two years later, said that his wife became spiritually distressed and depressed, although she had died with Christian fortitude. It cannot have been an easy time for the young children, although Miss Branwell had come up from Cornwall to alleviate the trouble and the pain.

The churchyard at Haworth bears eloquent testimony to the frequency of death at an early age in Victorian times, and Mr Brontë's religion no doubt ensured that the blow of his wife's death was met with courage. Yet the loss of their mother at such a time in the Brontë's lives was a cruel stroke, leaving them ill-equipped for the future, but with a craving for the love and affection of which they had been deprived. Mr Brontë did his best to find a substitute, but he was now over forty, and six small children cannot have been much of an attraction to any woman. Miss Branwell tried hard and Mr Brontë speaks warmly of her kindness to himself and the children. In *Jane Eyre* Jane's aunt is cruel, in *Shirley* Caroline Helstone's aunt is silly, but if anything Miss Branwell appears to have been more like Helen Huntingdon's aunt in *The Tenant of Wildfell Hall*, stern and sensible. As a Wesleyan Methodist Miss Branwell may have had mild disagreements with Mr Brontë on religious matters, but it is quite wrong to attribute to her any of the Calvinist doctrines of predeterminism to salvation and damnation, by which the Brontës appear from time to time to have been terrified.[3]

The decision to send the Brontë girls to school at Cowan Bridge was probably inspired by Miss Firth. Mr Brontë sent Maria and Elizabeth there on 1 July 1824, Charlotte on 10 August and Emily on 26 November. Maria left in ill health on 14 February 1825 and died 6 May, Elizabeth on 31 May to die on 15 June, while Charlotte and Emily left on 1 June. These dates, taken from the Cowan Bridge registers, would seem to indicate either that Mr Brontë was unduly negligent about his daughter's welfare, or that he was in general satisfied with arrangements at the school, sending Emily and Charlotte to join Elizabeth and Maria and keeping on the three younger girls after Maria had fallen ill. In Mrs Gaskell's account there is some confusion, and it is said that Charlotte and Emily stayed on after Elizabeth fell ill, but this is not so.

It is equally clear that Charlotte was not satisfied with the way the school was run, and that she thought the portrait of Lowood a fair and accurate form of revenge. She told Mrs Gaskell that Lowood was based on Cowan Bridge, and in the controversy over Cowan Bridge that followed the publication of Mrs Gaskell's life Mr Nicholls strictly maintained that his wife's fiction reflected the facts. In a revealing letter to W. S. Williams, Charlotte recounted with some enjoyment how a neighbouring clergyman had recognised Lowood and Mr Brocklehurst as portraits of Cowan Bridge and the Reverend Carus Wilson, and this does suggest that it was not just Charlotte who felt the resemblance.[4]

Charlotte was of course only eight when she was at Cowan Bridge and thirty when she wrote about it. Most people have rather a dim vision of their schooldays after twenty years, although Charlotte's memory was praised as being unusually good, and she said she remembered the school vividly. Most parents of imaginative children will know the experience of them exaggerating the foibles of their teachers in such a way that they are built up as monstrous tyrants, when on closer acquaintance these monsters turn out to be unassuming and hard working men and women. It is therefore right to allow for some element of exaggeration in Charlotte's account and to remember that *Jane Eyre* is not literal autobiography. There is no indication that Charlotte arrived under any cloud at the school; she was not in disgrace like Jane who had no sisters and stayed on at the school until she was grown up.

Cowan Bridge is the first of the many areas in Charlotte's life over which there is both controversy and confusion between life and literature. On the publication of Mrs Gaskell's life, friends and relatives of Carus Wilson rushed to his defence, and Mrs Gaskell was forced to modify her account. A dispute continued in the columns of the Yorkshire papers between Mr Nicholls and Mr Carus Wilson's son, engendering more heat than light. In 1857 Carus Wilson's son-in-law, the Reverend W. Shepheard, published a vindication of the Clergy Daughter's School. In this century further confusion has been caused by the discovery of a prospectus for Cowan Bridge, with most of the positions in the school held by members of the Carus Wilson family and including a scourgemistress to keep discipline. This, though believed by Margaret Lane, is almost certainly a forgery as none of the names correspond to the names of known teachers. It may have been produced at the time of the controversy. A certain amount of doubt still hangs over the testimony of teachers in favour of the school, reprinted in Mrs Gaskell's second edition, since if they came from people well represented in *Jane Eyre*, this would seem to be an argument in favour of Carus Wilson. But it seems fairly certain that the original of Miss Temple never wrote anything polite about the school, and most of the evidence comes from Miss Andrews, who appears in the novel in the less flattering role of Miss Scatcherd.[5]

The charges against the school can be summed up as follows. The students' health was neglected, with poor food and cold rooms exacerbating what was already an unhealthy situation; thus the fever which carries off poor Helen Burns in *Jane Eyre* and laid low Maria and Elizabeth Brontë as well as some other pupils was partly the school's fault. In addition, some of the teachers were unkind and unjust, with Carus Wilson condoning this injustice as a means of keeping the girls in a due state of humility. His own hypocrisy in demanding that the girls should dress simply, while his own family did not, is supposed to be condemned in the famous scene where Mr Brocklehurst's family visit the school in all their finery.

Medical knowledge was of course rather more primitive in 1824 than it is now, and it is to the credit of the school authorities that, as the Registers show, they recorded what infectious diseases the pupils had had. They also eventually moved the school to a more healthy situation at Casterton, although not until some years after the deaths of the two Brontës. Carus Wilson's son said there were only six deaths of fever in thirty-five years at Casterton and Cowan Bridge, and this seems to contradict the view that fever ravaged the school in 1825. Over the food there is conflicting testimony, although some admission by the Carus Wilson side that there had been an incompetent cook.

The published works of Carus Wilson do reveal a rather sinister sternness.[6] He seemed to take the view that to spare the rod was to spoil the child, that death was a blessed relief from painful life, and that existing social distinctions were divinely ordained. Like many Evangelicals, such as Wilberforce, Carus Wilson was both rich and a strong Tory. His object in founding the school was to train the daughters of poor clergymen to their station in life, namely to be governesses. Governess is stated in the Register to be the future career of both Maria and Elizabeth Brontë. To this end academic subjects, such as history, geography and French, were taught, as well as practical accomplishments such as needlework. In company with many other girls the Brontës were said to be very bad at these subjects, although Charlotte did very well at her next school, and Maria is usually supposed to have been clever. The harsh remarks about the low attainments of the Brontës at such a tender age may seem unfair, although it would seem that the school did, unlike many others at the time, have high standards.

Charlotte wrote *Jane Eyre*, a story about a governess, at a time when she had been unsuccessfully a governess, and when, with her father in poor health, it might seem that she would have to be a governess again. Her resentment and rebellion at the poor way governesses were treated may colour her account of the way governesses were trained. The rich, powerful and pompous Mr Brocklehurst prepares us for the rich, powerful and pompous Ingram family. The episode, however, where the wealthy and frivolous Brocklehurst family visit the school cannot be based on the Carus Wilson family. Carus Wilson's eldest daughter, the only one old enough to be shown off in any way in 1825, was at that time an invalid.[7]

Mr Brocklehurst is unkind to Jane, but Miss Scatcherd is cruel and unfair to Helen Burns. Helen is usually assumed to be based on Maria Brontë, although the death of Maria did not occur at the school, and Helen and Jane are of course not related. It is Mrs Gaskell who first identifies Helen with Maria, although Charlotte says that Helen is based on reality. We have tributes to Maria from Mr Brontë who said of her that during her illness she exhibited many symptoms of a heart under divine influence, and from Charlotte who spoke of her prematurely developed and remarkable intellect as well as the mildness, wisdom and fortitude of her character. Helen Burns exhibits these characteristics, although she is perhaps too mild. Charlotte in the same letter says she suffered to see her sisters perishing, and when she arrived at Roe Head some six years after Cowan Bridge she spoke of her dead sisters to Mary Taylor as wonders of talent and kindness.[8]

Jane Eyre misses Helen Burns as one of the few people who had been kind to her. And no doubt Maria's death left a gaping hole in the Brontë family, since as the eldest she had tried to take her mother's place. This role now had to be taken by Charlotte, always in future, protective, perhaps over-protective of Emily and Anne. With Branwell, not very much younger than her and with special privileges as the only boy of the family, the relationship was rather different. Branwell, whose education is a bit of a mystery, may have been at home when Maria died, and is likely to have felt her loss keenly although we should not perhaps make too much of later poems of his which have heroines called Maria or recount episodes which involve seeing a dead sister in a coffin.[9] Charlotte must have at first sight seemed a poor substitute, and there must have been a certain rivalry and resentment between the two siblings, although this rivalry produced fruitful literary results.

After leaving Cowan Bridge Charlotte remained at home for five and a half years. We have only one letter of hers during this period. She and her brother and sisters did begin writing at this time, and the writing as well as the high opinion that was formed of her work at her next school shows that the education she received at home was a good one. According to Mrs Gaskell it was Miss Branwell who instructed the children, but their father, who probably taught Branwell, talked to them of matters of political interest. They were encouraged to read on their own, and the visits to Ponden House library must have started.

When Charlotte arrived at her next school she knew little of geography or grammar, but a great deal about poetry and politics. She rapidly rose to first position in the class. Few could doubt her intellect and her capacity for hard work. Mr Brontë and Miss Branwell are likely to have fostered her talents, albeit in rather an unsystematic manner. Mr Brontë's enthusiasm for education has already been commented upon. The year at Cowan Bridge, in spite of its charitable status had, unless he received some help, cost him almost half his income as well as the lives of two of his daughters, but is unlikely to have dimmed that enthusiasm.

There were of course some handicaps to learning. In spite of his tragic losses Mr Brontë's family was still a large one which had to be fitted into a relatively small house. Shared bedrooms meant a lack of privacy. Children of today who demand their own room and sometimes a private bathroom as well would have found it hard to cope with the one outside privy and the water brought up in jugs. Charlotte's shortsightedness and the lack of artificial light must have restricted reading hours; comparative poverty and the remoteness of Haworth restricted reading matter.

The reading of the Brontës is a difficult subject. We have the catalogue of the Ponden House library to which they had access, and of the Keighley Mechanics' Institute to which they may have had access. Neither library was exactly near and neither was strong on contemporary fiction. In 1831 Miss Branwell agreed to take *Fraser's Magazine*, apparently in place of *Blackwood's Magazine*. Mr Brontë would have subscribed to a local newspaper. Mrs Brontë had some copies of *The Ladies' Magazine* sent up from Cornwall, and Mr Brontë must have had a few books from his classical and religious studies, some of which have survived till this day. Mrs Gaskell recounts how Mr Brontë disapproved of *The Ladies' Magazine* as recounting foolish love stories, but this seems the only attempt made by him to censor his children's reading. Queen Victoria had yet to come to the throne, and there was little concern about works likely to bring a blush to the cheek of a young person.

There were of course many encouragements towards study in the Brontë household. There was not much else to do. Servants did most of the housework. The Garrs sisters, Nancy and Sarah, who had followed the Brontës from Thornton had been replaced during Mrs Brontë's final illness by a temporary nurse, a lady who fed Mrs Gaskell with much erroneous information, but Sarah Garrs remained in service with the Brontës, and at some stage in the 1820s the Brontës were joined by the faithful Tabitha, or Tabby, Aykroyd who in spite of failing health stayed with the household until she died shortly before Charlotte. We hear in Emily's first birthday note of bedwork and peeling potatoes, but this cannot have been strenuous.

Other entertainments were in short supply. There was walking on the moors. Pets came into the household gradually in the 1830s. We have already seen how the Brontës had few friends in Haworth. Miss Branwell never really got used to Yorkshire ways. Mr Brontë's shortage of friends is perhaps shown by the fact that the same people had to act as godparent to more than one child. Of his clerical acquaintances, the Morgans would appear to have been childless, and Charlotte did not like Mr Morgan, the Atkinsons also had no children, and the Franks children were too young. Nearer home, the rector of Keighley, the Reverend Theodore Dury, did have children, but this household was likely to be a little grand for the Brontës, since Mr Dury was a patron of Cowan Bridge and related through marriage to Charlotte's first employers, the Sidgwicks.

Inevitably, and not unhappily, the Brontë children were forced upon each other for company. The members of this close-knit family had to be both very restrained in finding entertainment without getting in each other's way, and to be very imaginative in getting the best from the limited resources for entertainment at their disposal. At an early stage in their lives the seeds were sown for that strange mixture of stern repression of the feelings and wild outbursts of the imagination which characterise both the works and the lives of the Brontës.

At the beginning of 1831 Charlotte was sent to school at Roe Head. This was a very different kind of school from Cowan Bridge, but it is not exactly clear why Mr Brontë should have decided once again to send his daughters away from home. It has been suggested that he had been ill, and was anxious to provide for his eldest daughter in case he should die. It has also been suggested that the Atkinsons paid the fees. There is no evidence for either suggestion, although the proximity of the Atkinsons, the Franks and other old friends from Dewsbury days may have inspired the move – a fortunate one for Charlotte and for her biographers, since she made friends there, and it is from her letters to one of these friends that we derive most of our knowledge of her life.

Miss Wooler ran the school with the aid of her sisters. She seems to have been a competent and kind woman, with whom Charlotte remained on good terms for the whole of her life, eventually taking the unusual step of asking Miss Wooler to give her away when she married Mr Nicholls. There were tensions when Charlotte returned to Roe Head as a teacher, but these were perhaps inevitable, given Charlotte's lack of ability in this role and the fact that most teachers find themselves on occasions disagreeing with their headmistresses or headmasters. In both *The Professor* and *Villette* Charlotte imagines her heroines running a successful school of their own, and she wanted to do the same with her sisters. Such a school would have been like that of Miss Wooler.

Charlotte, in spite of starting with certain disadvantages, soon emerged at the head of her class and bore off three prizes. Intellectual competition may not have been very severe. Unlike at Cowan Bridge there was no particular reason for the girls to be trained up as governesses. Some of the girls, like Amelia Walker, niece of the Atkinsons, had no reason to believe that they would ever be asked to do anything, as their parents were rich. Also in this position were Leah and Mary Brooke; but their father's banking business failed, forcing Mary Brooke to seek a position of some kind. The aunt of the Brookes was married to Mr Brontë's old vicar at Dewsbury at Buckworth who died in 1835 to be succeeded by Miss Wooler's brother-in-law the Reverend Thomas Allbutt, and the Brookes may have been related to another of Miss Wooler's brother-in-laws, the Reverend Edward Carter.

These comfortable clerical connections are stressed because, though Charlotte was excluded from them, in her books she tends to make everyone either known or be related to everyone else rather too easily. Her two closest friends, Mary Taylor and Ellen Nussey, were themselves distantly related, and they had connections with a great many of the other people whom Charlotte mentions in her letters, some of whom had been or were to be pupils at Roe Head.

The background of Ellen Nussey and Mary Taylor was perhaps not quite as secure as that of some other pupils, or as some biographers have tried to suggest. The identification of the Taylor family with the Yorkes of *Shirley* is better established than most of the connections made between Charlotte's fiction and fact, and certainly the unnecessary excursus on the death of Jessie Yorke must be a reflection of the death of Mary Taylor's sister, Martha, in Belgium. Mary Taylor assumed that the Yorkes were her family, but reported that her mother and her brother disagreed and said that the likeness was not a faithful one. The Yorkes appear as eccentric and radical; the Red House at Gomersal where the Taylors lived is a fairly comfortable one, but the Taylors do not seem to have been particularly well provided for. Mary and Martha's move to Belgium, which pointed the Brontës in the same direction, would seem to have arisen from the same motive – a wish to obtain qualifications for some profession. As it was, Mary emigrated with her cousin Ellen to New Zealand, and in well-edited subsequent correspondence emerges as a strong-minded independent and admirable woman.[10] Very unfortunately little of her correspondence with Charlotte survives. Had more done so we might have seen the Brontës in rather a different light. Certainly her account of the time at Roe Head, concentrating as it does on Charlotte's intellectual attainments, is a great deal more interesting than that of Ellen Nussey which is principally concerned with dress and deportment.

Ellen Nussey is a vital figure in the Brontë story, and we must be grateful to her for preserving so many of Charlotte's letters. Her confused and confusing efforts to publish these letters, her jealousy of Mrs Gaskell, and her dislike of Mr Nicholls and Mr Brontë tend to diminish our gratitude, although we only see these aspects of her character after Charlotte's death.[11] She tends to emerge in some Brontë biographies as the heroine of a Jane Austen-like novel, living in a grand house and going on visits to Bath. Curiously, like Jane Austen she lived with her sister and mother, had two brothers who were clergymen, one called Henry, and one brother called George who was mad. These coincidental resemblances are unimportant because unlike Jane Austen Ellen Nussey appears to have been neither witty nor particularly intelligent.

Nor was her social position so secure. References by Charlotte in an early letter to Rydings as one of the family seats of England, and by Ellen herself to its grandeur tend to conceal the fact that the Nussey's stay in Rydings was of short duration, and they only rented the house anyway. No doubt the house seemed grand to Charlotte. One of Ellen's brothers was a doctor of some distinction and hence there were visits to Bath and London, but Jane Austen unkindly and snobbishly would have pointed out the number of Ellen Nussey's relatives who were not very successfully engaged in trade. Ellen Nussey does not seem to have done very much with her life, although she did once contemplate taking up a position as companion to some people in Suffolk.

Most of Charlotte's more interesting letters to Ellen Nussey came in the early period when with passionate intensity she poured out her feelings of sinfulness and recommended books to her. Thereafter the letters are more reserved. There is no mention of Monsieur Heger or the writing of *Jane Eyre*. The courtship with Mr Nicholls is alluded to in veiled terms, although gaps in the correspondence make it likely that Ellen suppressed some letters on this point. Much of Charlotte's correspondence is taken up with trivial gossip or information and enquiries about health which are hardly illuminating.

Husband-hunting is another major preoccupation of the letters. Although portraits of Ellen Nussey show her as a pretty girl, she never seemed to get very far with her admirers. In the circles in which Ellen moved one tended to marry one's cousins or the brothers of one's friends, and in fact Henry Nussey did propose to Charlotte Brontë, and Mary Taylor's brother married Amelia Ringrose, a girl previously engaged to the mad George Nussey. But students of Brontë novels will not find many traces of Mr Rochester in the middle of the tittle-tattle about these courtships.

Given the unexciting nature of Ellen's personality it seems odd that Charlotte should have been drawn to her. The passionate nature of some of her early statements like 'my darling, I have lavished the warmest affections of a very hot, tenacious heart upon you' and the expressions of self-loathing in 'trying to do right, checking wrong feelings, repressing wrong thoughts' might suggest something unnatural in the friendship, and we cannot dismiss the idea entirely.[12] Starved of love Charlotte craved for someone who could both love and be loved, and Ellen Nussey, whom we see in old age as querulous and pathetic, almost certainly in youth had an appealing quality which Charlotte found hard to resist. It is possible that Charlotte's guilt arose from other reasons; adolescent religion as well as adolescent sexuality can cause difficulties. Charlotte was prepared for confirmation at Roe Head by the Reverend Edward Carter, brother-in-law to Miss Wooler. In addition she was distressed by her ability to lose herself in the world of her imagination, to which the next chapter will be devoted. Charlotte's psychological difficulties would have provided a rich field for an adolescent counsellor or modern psychologist; without these aids, Charlotte's strength of character enabled her to survive.

It would be interesting to know more about the syllabus Charlotte followed at Roe Head, presumably much the same as that she taught when she returned four years later as a teacher. We do have a few of her schoolbooks. Some of these, like Rollin's *History*, appear in the list of books that Charlotte recommends to Ellen Nussey four years later, and this is a little odd since Ellen and Charlotte had presumably studied together – perhaps Ellen was not a very good student. Charlotte's proficiency at Scripture, not perhaps surprising in the daughter of a clergyman, was noted by Mary Taylor. Her French, whose faults in a letter to Ellen Nussey of 1833 are conspicuous, almost certainly improved while she was at Roe Head, although she did know some French before she went to school, making a remarkably successful translation of Voltaire's *Henriade* as early as 11 May 1830.

The work at Roe Head is unlikely to have taxed Charlotte unduly. Young ladies of the time were not expected to be stretched very far, and Charlotte's companions do not seem to have been academically very ambitious. It is therefore not surprising that she should have done well at the school, especially since she had, as was probably unknown to Miss Wooler, already undergone an apprenticeship in writing, usually considered to be far more important in forming the novelist than her school curriculum. Charlotte received little formal schooling, but schools and education do play a large part in her novels and more work should be done on this subject.

3
Writer

There has been no shortage of work on Charlotte's juvenile writings. Mrs Gaskell was aware of their existence, but not of their significance. Mr Nicholls took them with him back to Ireland, and then Clement Shorter and T. J. Wise got hold of them. This led to the manuscripts being widely scattered and a whole series of unsatisfactory printed editions being issued. Only in the last few years, largely thanks to the labours of Dr Christine Alexander, have Charlotte's juvenilia been sorted out, and we can soon look forward to proper editions of everything Charlotte wrote.[1]

Even with these editions we will still be in difficulties with the juvenilia. When only part of the juvenilia was available, scholars tended to exaggerate the literary merit of what Charlotte wrote, to find biographical information from the uncertain evidence of poetry and fiction, incompletely edited and dated, and above all to find parallels with Charlotte's novels. Most of these claims can now be seen to be false. Much of what Charlotte wrote without publication in mind is incoherent and unrealistic, ill spelt and insufficiently punctuated, with cardboard characters and melodramatic plots. Biographical parallels are hard to draw – even when we have got the dates right – between a schoolgirl and governess quietly leading a humdrum existence in Yorkshire and adulterous aristocrats cavorting in an improbably magnificent African setting. Finally, although the juvenilia do contain a few features of the later work, such as masterful heroes, lonely orphans, resolute governesses, quarrelling brothers and mad wives, they contain so much less than the mature novels that it cheapens our appreciation of the novels if we compare the two. *The Professor* has obvious similarities with *Villette*, but apart from this resemblance Charlotte's novels are very different from each other. The assumption that Charlotte could only write one novel, namely the story of her life, is an unfair one. Although her talent was not as wide ranging as that of Dickens, being indeed much closer to that of Thackeray – who is also sometimes accused of being only able to write one novel – Charlotte's art did grow as she grew older, and it is almost insulting to look for parallels between the juvenilia and the mature novels. We do not look in *Pickwick Papers* for parallels with *Bleak House*.

And yet the juvenilia must be discussed by any biographer of Charlotte. They do indicate her ideas and her concerns and give precious information on the sources of her inspiration. Moreover most of them were written during the period when the only other source of information that we have is the series of rather stilted letters to Ellen Nussey. It is also unlikely that without the previous apprenticeship in writing the Brontës would ever have been able to write the novels that they did.

Attempts have been made to fit all the stories written by Charlotte into a consecutive pattern. The fact that Branwell as well as Charlotte was involved in the stories, that they involved verse as well as prose, and that both Branwell and Charlotte shuttled to and fro in time and space, reviving or killing off a character as it suited them, makes such an attempt virtually impossible. With Emily and Anne, who worked on a separate narrative about a realm called Gondal, we have only the evidence of the poems – too little evidence for us to reconstruct a coherent narrative – but with Charlotte and Branwell there is almost too much material.

Chronology is important. The purchase of some wooden soldiers by Mr Brontë in 1826 was the signal for the Brontës to start imagining stories about them, although nothing in writing survives before 1829. Originally all four children were involved in making up stories, but Emily and Anne broke away to form their own cycle of tales sometime before 1834. Charlotte and Branwell continued writing stories and verse about their imaginary realm until 1839. This realm is usually known as Angria, although the actual foundation of the breakaway state of Angria did not take place until the end of 1833. The collaboration between Branwell and Charlotte was fitful, not helped by their frequent absences from each other, their different interests, an initial rivalry as to who was in charge, and finally a recognition by Charlotte of Branwell's failings. At times, however, we see a certain common purpose between the two authors, and it is sometimes difficult to distinguish which author is responsible for which new element in the saga.

On 12 March 1829 Charlotte wrote as follows: 'Our plays were established: Young Men, June 1826; Our fellows, July 1827; Islanders, December 1827. These are our great plays that are not kept secret. Emily's and my bed plays were established, December 1,

1827; the others March 1828. Bed plays mean secret plays; they are very nice ones.'[2]

Such were the small beginnings for the Brontës' literary endeavours. We know nothing of the bed plays and little of Our Fellows, but the Young Men and Islanders soon merged into a story of a group of English warriors founding a new colony in Africa. The Duke of Wellington featured prominently in this story. He was Prime Minister of England at the time, thirteen years after the defeat of Napoleon at Waterloo. His two sons, the Marquess of Douro and Lord Charles Wellesley gradually took over his primary role in Charlotte's fiction, although some of the early stories concern actual political events of the time with references to Catholic emancipation and the prospects of Reform. Charlotte showed considerable hostility to Catholics and to Reform in *Tales of the Islanders*, volume 1, written in 1829. Blackwood's *Young Men's Magazine*, an attempt made in minuscule handwriting to imitate *Blackwood's Magazine*, had a great many references to political affairs.

The energy and ingenuity which the young Brontës put into these magazines at a time when Charlotte was only fourteen must amaze us. The tiny handwriting, the despair of the modern researcher, was an attempt to imitate real print, although the Brontës were always economical with paper. Articles about painters and actual illustrations in the magazines show their interest in art. Branwell tried to become a portrait painter, and at one stage Charlotte was working up to nine hours a day practising drawing.[3] The literary quality of the early stories is not high, and is usually strongly derivative, but even in her earliest stories Charlotte – inspired by romantic painters, such as Martin – was able to draw pictures in words.

Realism was slightly lacking in Charlotte's descriptions, set in Africa, of the aristocratic palaces of the Great Glass Town confederacy, otherwise known as Verreopolis or Verdopolis, where Charlotte and Branwell placed their adventures. They had some knowledge of African geography from articles in *Blackwood's Magazine* and books by Mungo Park in the Ponden House library, but the Africa they painted was full of English architecture from the Regency period. Another unrealistic feature of the adolescent writing is the tiresome way the four chief genii, standing for the four Brontë children, can dispose of or revive characters at will. A certain awkwardness about the narrator is present even in the adult novels.

Like *Blackwood's Magazine*, the early writing contained a certain amount of poetry, as well as both fiction and discussions on public affairs. Charlotte's poems never reach great heights, but some of the early ones show considerable skill in handling rhyme and metre as well as considerable reading of other poets. The eighteenth century as well as the Romantics influenced her. In the letter to Ellen Nussey recommending poetry she mentions Milton, Shakespeare, Thomson, Goldsmith, Pope, Scott, Byron, Campbell, Wordsworth and Southey. It was apparently too early for Keats and Shelley. Charlotte had certain reservations about Pope, whom she says she does not admire, and about Shakespeare and Byron on grounds of their potential indecency. In her own early poems Wordsworth and Thomson are the most prominent influences.

At a fairly early stage Charlotte discovered the attractions of love as a topic in both prose and poetry. It is not true to say that Charlotte totally abandoned the tedious fields of war and politics to Branwell while she explored the mysteries of the human heart, but Branwell's interest lay more in the former field, and Charlotte's in the latter.[4] Charlotte's principal hero Arthur, the Marquess of Douro, appears early in her tales, and we learn of his love for the daughter of his father's doctor, Marion Hume. There was in fact a real love-affair between the real Marquess of Douro, elder son of the Duke of Wellington, and Elizabeth Hume, daughter of Wellington's doctor, although Charlotte's imagination soon takes over from reality. Branwell originally took sides with the French, and we find him adopting the persona of Young Soult, the son of one of Napoleon's generals, although later his principal hero, arch-rival to Douro, is Alexander Rogue, later Viscount Ellrington and Earl of Northangerland. Douro, likewise promoted to Duke of Zamorna and King of Angria, fights battles and is involved in political intrigue, but we are mainly interested in his amorous escapades, whereas Northangerland's amours are principally in the past and we hear more of his attempts to gain power.

Charlotte uses as a narrator for several of her earlier works, Lord Charles Wellesley, the name of Wellington's younger son. He is more lyrical and satirical than his elder brother, but is also interested in the supernatural. Two early stories unconnected with *The Glass Town Saga*, *An Adventure in Ireland* (28 April 1829), and *The Adventures of Ernest Alembert* (25 May 1830) are connected with fairies and witchcraft. Charlotte was fascinated by the way her fictional characters emerged as real people in her visions, then faded as if in a dream. Later this borderline between fiction and reality was to become a worrying obsession with her, and later still her mature novels retain vestiges of this earlier anxiety. In a famous but often misinterpreted poem 'The trumpet hath sounded' (11 December 1831) she appears to have foreseen that eventually she would have to escape from the world of the juvenilia.

> The secrets of genii my tongue may not tell
> But hoarsely they murmured: 'Bright city, farewell'
> Then melted away like a dream of the night
> While their palace evanished in oceans of light.[5]

Glass Town was not destroyed, but at some stage between 1831 and 1834 Anne and Emily started their own cycle of stories, the concept of the genii was abandoned, and by the beginning of 1834 Charlotte and Branwell had worked out a new avenue for their energies with the creation of the Kingdom of Angria, won by the inhabitants of Verdopolis after a war with the neighbouring Ashantees. In stories previous to this Charlotte, while principally concerned with the loves of Douro and his growing rivalry for Rogue, has some other themes. Branwell had imagined a revolution in Verdopolis – recent events in France had fired his interests – and we find Charlotte in *Something About Arthur* (1833) mentioning an attack on a mill, about which she must have heard when she was at Roe Head and to which she was to return in *Shirley*. In the same story Mina Laury, a girl of humble birth but long-standing devotion to Douro, nearly marries him. In *The Foundling*, written in the same year, two new characters, Sydney and Lady Julia Wellesley are introduced; here it is the man who appears to be of humble ancestry, although he is later discovered to be of suitably noble birth. The eventual marriage between Julia and Sydney does not work, as Julia is a spoilt aristocrat. So is Lady Zenobia Ellrington whose violent passion for Douro – in spite of her marriage to Rogue, to whom she gives her title – is also recorded in *The Foundling*. In *The Green Dwarf* (2 September 1833) Charlotte delves back into the past of Alexander Percy, alias Rogue. Though more sinister than Douro, Rogue has certain shared Byronic characteristics. It is difficult to keep track of his many wives and mistresses. In *Lily Hart* (7 December 1833) we hear of the secret courtship of the Duke of Fidena and Lily Hart, possibly inspired by the story of the relationship between Nelson and Lady Hamilton.

It is true that the principal work of 1833 for Charlotte was *Arthuriana*, a collection of six tales and three poems in which Douro figures prominently. The narrator of these tales is Lord Charles Wellesley, and fraternal jealousy makes him speak of Douro's increasing dissipation and degeneracy. Douro is harsh to his wife and haughty to others, but as yet, unlike Rogue, not actually corrupt and adulterous. Adultery is, however, a subject to which both Charlotte and Branwell refer to quite lightly, and this may seem odd in view of the fact that they were innocent adolescents who had hardly emerged from their nineteenth-century parsonage. We must remember, however, that Queen Victoria had not come to the throne, and that inveterate adulterers like Lord Melbourne and the Duke of Wellington still held the public stage. On issues of sexual morality public taste changed almost as much between 1833 and 1847, when *Jane Eyre* created such a shock, as it has in the reverse direction between 1953 and 1967.

Charlotte and Branwell, of course, derived their information about both adultery and the aristocracy from books and not from real life. We have one glimpse of them in the real world at this time, and it shows them in a very different light from that in which the heroes of the juvenilia appear. In July 1833 Ellen Nussey came to stay briefly in Haworth, and in September of the same year the Brontës joined with the Nusseys in making a visit to Bolton Abbey. Ellen's published account of these two visits stresses the quaintness of the Brontë home and even hints at the eccentricity of Branwell's behaviour. Her unpublished notes are more severe. They show the shyness of the Brontës, their inability to get on with people at Haworth, the strangeness of their appearance, and their gaucherie when confronted with the hardly formidable Nussey family.[6]

Charlotte's relations with Branwell are interesting. She seems to have co-operated with him in establishing the basic framework of the story, although there are differences in emphasis and detail. Occasional obscure literary jokes may be directed by one author against another. In an early story Branwell introduces his three sisters without any disguise into his narrative, and speaks of them with a good deal of contempt. In *My Angria and the Angriuns* (October 1834) Charlotte caricatures Branwell in Patrick Benjamin Wiggins as 'a low slightly built man, a bush of canary yellow hair and a pair of spectacles placed across a prominent Roman nose'. These comic jibes are perfectly compatible with a happy affection between brother and sister, marred perhaps by occasional rivalries with Charlotte the eldest child and Branwell the only boy. Branwell had a superior education and considerable talent, as his poetry shows; he was also, it seems, a little better than his sisters at mixing with people in Haworth, even though this may have involved dubious company in such haunts as The Black Bull public house. But it is a mistake to exaggerate Charlotte's admiration for and devotion to her brother; there is a considerable gap between Branwell's appearance, both insignificant and eccentric, and 'the towering overbearingly lofty' figure of Zamorna.

Douro becomes Zamorna, and Rogue/Percy becomes Northangerland in the stories of 1834. A new kingdom called Angria, won as a result of wars against the French and the Ashantees, was established to the east of Verdopolis. Zamorna and Northangerland were two of the pioneers of this kingdom, and Douro was made Duke of Zamorna, while Rogue, already Viscount Ellrington through marriage, became Earl of Northangerland. This confusing multiplicity of titles was further complicated by the fact that Zamorna became King, even at times Emperor, of Angria and Northangerland his Prime Minister. More importantly the two heroes are further linked by the marriage of Northangerland's daughter, Mary Percy, to Zamorna.

Marian Hume, always rather a shadowy figure, seems to have been killed off early in 1834 and by the time of *High Life in Verdopolis* (20 February–20 March 1833) the more spirited Mary seems to have replaced her. Marian's death is said to have been due to a broken heart in *A Peep into a Picture Book* (30 May 1834), and in *High Life in Verdopolis* Douro's Byronic ways are exaggerated. Mary had every reason to feel jealousy and despair, as Zamorna's illicit amours now feature in almost every story. It is a mistake to accuse Zamorna of instant unfaithfulness to his new wife, as in the stories of 1834 Charlotte moved freely in time, sometimes, for example in *A Leaf from an Unopened Volume* (17 January 1834), imagining Angria as having been founded for twenty-five years with Zamorna having a grown-up son, sometimes, as in *A Brace of Characters* (30 October 1834), referring back to past amours and marriages of Zamorna. In *The Spell* (21 June–21 July 1834) Zamorna has a twin brother, perhaps a convenient device for expressing Charlotte's mixed feelings towards her hero, whose irregular liasons both delighted and shocked her. The plot in the stories of this time is always thin, and the titles of some of the collections which Charlotte made, like *Corner Dishes* and *A Scrap Book*, indicate that she was quite unable to weld her thoughts into a coherent pattern. Later, when at Roe Head as a teacher, Charlotte became distinctly worried by the way her inspiration seemed to take hold of her without reason, and even her verse becomes incoherent.

In 1834 and 1835 one controlling factor in the Brontës' lives appears to have been politics. They are a recurring theme in the letters to Ellen Nussey of this period. Ellen would by all accounts seem to have been an unthinking conservative. In letters of 1834 when Ellen was staying in London Charlotte refers enviously to 'the splendours and novelties' of that great city which must have seemed such a contrast to 'the solitude of our wild little hill village', and asks not about parties and dresses, but whether Ellen has seen any of the 'Great Personages' whom the sitting of Parliament now detains in London.[7] In the first of Emily's and Anne's diary fragments on 24 November 1834 a reference to Sir Robert Peel standing for Leeds occurs incongruously between the feeding of the animals and peeling potatoes. Then in 1835 Charlotte refers to the 'course Politics are taking'.[8]

There had been a political crisis in 1834. The Whigs, after coming to power and passing the Reform Bill in 1832, found themselves divided in 1834, largely over Irish policy. The King, William IV, had invited the Tory Sir Robert Peel to form a ministry, but it had been frequently defeated. In 1835 a new election was called, and the Tories – much to the disappointment of Charlotte and of Mr Brontë, who had supported them – were defeated.

It is strange that enthusiasm for finding real life equivalents for the characters in Charlote Brontë's novels has not extended to the heroes in her juvenilia. Kings George IV and William IV, though amorous, were hardly romantic characters, but William IV did play some part in the constitutional crises of the early 1830s, and these are reflected in the struggles of Angria. Zamorna certainly owes something to the Duke of Wellington; autocratic and unhappily married, the Duke was in opposition for much of the 1830s, but wielded considerable authority. His wife had died in 1831, and in a good Angrian incident which seems improbable to students of modern politics an angry mob had besieged the Duke's house at the time her body lay there. Wellington's extra-marital affairs were notorious, although when and how Charlotte would become aware of them is not clear. She might have read the memoirs of Harriette Wilson at any time after 1825.[9] In the case of Northangerland there are certain parallels with Wellington's liberal opponent, Lord Melbourne, although Northangerland's many wives and mistresses are less exciting than Melbourne's wife, the notorious Lady Caroline Lamb. Sir Robert Peel, Prime Minister in 1834 with Wellington's support, seems both in character and position rather like Howard Warner, the faithful ally of Zamorna.

Lady Caroline Lamb's most famous lover was Byron, and Byron's poetry and life have many echoes in the juvenilia. Moore's life of Byron had appeared in 1830, and although Charlotte pretended to be shocked by it and by 'Don Juan' in the letter of July 1834 giving advice to Ellen Nussey, she certainly had read both. The innocence of some of the ladies, such as Haidée in 'Don Juan', and the worldliness of others, such as Donna Elivira, is reflected in the stories of Angria which derives something of its African landscape from the gentler shores of the Mediterranean. Branwell, whose poetry sometimes involves direct plagiarism of Byron, is likely to have been interested in Byron's political views, and Douro is concerned with literature as well as politics. Byron's difficulties with his wife and the world-weariness of his heroes are the most obvious links between him and both Douro and Northangerland.

One of Charlotte's later heroines,Caroline Vernon, in a tale written in 1839 says that the four best men that ever lived were 'Lord Byron and Bonaparte, the Duke of Wellington and Lord Edward Fitzgerald'. The latter, a rebellious and aristocratic Irishman, had also been the subject of a biography by Moore. Charlotte is unlikely to have shared Caroline's opinions. She certainly did not admire Napoleon, and there is a poem stating how France had been ruined by him.[10] Her admiration for Byron and the Byronic hero is mixed with distaste. Between 1835 and 1839 the stress between these two sorts of feeling almost caused a breakdown, although Charlotte had other worries as well. Before 1835 the constant creations of new characters and incidents, with the fertile imagination of Branwell always at work, meant that Charlotte's writing was undisturbed by any crisis of conscience, although it was uncontrolled and she was unable to penetrate the complexities of her characters.

With the move as governess at Roe Head on 29 July 1835 the second great crisis of Charlotte's life, after the trauma of Lowood, was about to arrive. It is impossible not to feel sorry that the happy and united home of the Brontës with all four children at home had to be broken up. The family was not at home together, except for short intervals, until 1845 in the very different circumstances of Branwell's disgrace and Charlotte's heart-break. From these searing experiences sprang the novels of the Brontës; the happy years at home produced the rather pitiful early juvenilia. Charlotte's next creative period was just as pitiful but more interesting.

4
Teacher

The years 1835–40 are important but unhappy ones for all the Brontës. Charlotte spent most of her time teaching, not very cheerfully, at Miss Wooler's school and made her first unsuccessful attempt to be a governess. Branwell was faced with considerable setbacks in his aspirations to be an artist, and, like Charlotte, received discouragement in his literary ambitions. Emily made two brief forays from home, as a pupil at Miss Wooler's and as a teacher at Miss Patchett's school near Halifax; on both occasions she suffered from homesickness. Anne was ill and unhappy at Miss Wooler's school, and her first attempt to be a governess was as unfortunate as Charlotte's.

Writing about this period some years later, Ellen Nussey blamed Mr Brontë, whom she disliked, for thrusting his daughters into a career for which they were totally unsuited.[1] It is true that the Brontës were not good teachers, and that teaching at that time was not a profession with many rewards. On the other hand, as the Brontës were later drearily to recount in their books, it was about the only profession for which they were qualified, and it is difficult to accuse Mr Brontë of anything more than a certain degree of unworldly optimism in thinking that all would be well. This is shown in a letter to Mrs Franks in 1835 when Charlotte first returned to Roe Head. In this letter Mr Brontë refers to a recent bout of ill health. This may have prompted him to seek to provide for his daughters who would have no money after his death.[2]

The only other career open to the Brontës was matrimony; in this period Charlotte received two proposals of marriage, and there arrived at Haworth the Reverend William Weightman, a cheerful curate, who in an ordinary Victorian novel – and even in ordinary life – would have made an ideal husband for any of the Brontë sisters. *Agnes Grey* is an ordinary novel, but we do not know for certain whether it reflects reality. We do not know much about Charlotte's two suitors, but Charlotte was not an ordinary Victorian young lady, and the impetuosity of the Irish Mr Pryce, and the calculated proposal of Ellen's brother Henry did not appeal to her.

Nevertheless love and loneliness, romantic dreams and the humdrum reality of life as a teacher play a large part in Charlotte's novels, and it is therefore important that we chart the years 1835–40 fairly carefully, especially as her juvenile writings during this period – now freer from Branwell's influence – provide useful insights into her future concerns as a novelist. Unfortunately these years, as well as being unhappy ones for the Brontës, have proved to be unhappy for Brontë biographers, the main difficulty being chronology. Many of Charlotte's poems in this period are undated. Her letters to Ellen Nussey, delivered very often by hand, and before the invention of the postal service, have been dated wrongly.

Fortunately the chronology of this period has been largely sorted out owing to the labours of Dr Edward Chitham.[3] The key date is that of the letter in which Charlotte writes of the departure of Emily as a teacher to Law Hill. Charlotte absent-mindedly wrote the date as 2 October 1836. Subsequent editors and biographers have accepted this as a mistake, and changed the date to 2 October 1837. The postmark of the letter, delivered in the days before the penny post, but when a primitive local post had been established, is in fact 6 October 1838.

Once this date has been established, several, but not all, of the other dates in this period fall into place. It looks as if Charlotte may have stayed at Miss Wooler's until the end of 1838, although spending some time at home in the summer because of ill health. The move of Miss Wooler's school from Roe Head to Dewsbury Moor may not have taken place until 1838, and Anne Brontë who soon replaced Emily as a student may not have seen Dewsbury Moor, since she appears to have become ill at Roe Head, and returned home in 1837. Ellen Nussey's family moved at some stage from the grand Rydings to the humbler Brookroyd, but we cannot date this move exactly. Ellen's visits to her brother John in London and Bath would appear to have taken place in 1837 and 1838, although we do not know if she returned home in the meantime.

Charlotte's letters to Ellen are slightly less frequent and less informative in the period Ellen was away from home, but a great deal of poetry and some juvenile stories, also difficult to date, supply us with additional information about Charlotte's state of mind. This does not seem to have been a happy one, although Charlotte had certain advantages. Miss Wooler's school was a good one and Charlotte was familiar with both teachers and curriculum. Her friends, the Taylors and Ellen Nussey, lived nearby, and for some of the time Charlotte had the company of her two sisters – although Anne and Emily were also miserable at Roe Head. However, Charlotte was not as lonely as Jane Eyre or Lucy Snowe.

Unlike Jane or Lucy, or for that matter William Crimsworth, who after initial difficulties establish themselves as successful teachers, Charlotte herself would have seemed to have found teaching difficult. Her small size and insignificant appearance cannot have helped, although many brilliant teachers have overcome similar disadvantages by the force of their personality. Charlotte too had a forceful personality, but she does not seem to have been particularly fond of children, and children are likely to have responded by not liking her. There are irritated complaints about her pupils in her letters. In her novels children – apart from little Adèle and the young Polly Hume, both of whom seem rather silly – do not feature very prominently. The schools in *The Professor* and *Villette* presumably reflect Belgium rather than Yorkshire, but Charlotte does not show much love for the young in those two novels. Miss Wooler's school is hardly likely to have been particularly enlightened or progressive, and Charlotte's originality must have found rote learning depressing. There is an interesting if obscure reference to the dreadful fifth section of Repetitions.[4]

In addition, Charlotte appears to have been painfully and not very attractively aware of her inferior social position as a teacher. This was particularly conspicuous when she became a governess with families whom she despised while they treated her as little better than a servant; Charlotte's rancour at this treatment was later to bear fruit in her novels. But even at Miss Wooler's, Charlotte was quick to take offence. She cannot have been pleased as she returned to the scene of her schooldays to find her stupider contemporaries enjoying life as ladies of leisure, while she was engaged in painful drudgery.

There were other troubles too; other members of the Brontë family were in a bad way. We do not know much about Emily's stay at Roe Head except that it was a short one. Anne lasted longer, but her ill health and religious depression must have caused anxiety, and Charlotte, who was teaching in order to pay for Anne's fees, appears to have been very angry with Miss Wooler for her behaviour and she almost left the school when Anne did. Branwell too was beginning to give cause for concern. In May 1835 when Charlotte wrote to Ellen Nussey, explaining that the family was about to split up, it was anticipated that Branwell would go to the Royal Academy in London to earn his living as a painter. We do not know when this visit took place, or how and why it was a failure. In September 1835 we find Mr Brontë paying the fees of a Mr Robinson in Bradford for instructing Branwell, and this was presumably before the débâcle. At the end of the same year Branwell began besieging *Blackwood's Magazine* with poetry and suggestions that they took him on as a contributor or reviewer. From this we may infer that it was at the end of 1835 that Branwell attempted to abandon art for literature, and thus that the foray to London took place in the autumn of 1835. In the event Branwell's literary aspirations were fruitless, and although he tried to revise his juvenile poems in 1837, in 1838 we find him embarking on a not very profitable career as a portrait painter in Bradford.[5]

Some of Branwell's heavy daubs survive, and in fact show less talent than his poetry which is marred by an excess of Byronic gloom and a certain amount of plagiarism. We do not know what happened; Branwell's fictional account in one of his stories of a young painter visiting a metropolis and dissipating his money on small squibs of rum need not necessarily be autobiographical, any more than Charlotte's story *Henry Hastings*, written in the spring of 1839, must be an accurate reflection of Charlotte's feelings towards her brother. Mrs Gaskell anticipated Branwell's decline into drunkeness in order to cast a smokescreen over Charlotte's love for Monsieur Heger, and Miss Gerin errs in thinking that the juvenile stories provide concrete evidence for Branwell's downfall and Charlotte's disillusion. Nevertheless at an early stage, though Branwell cannot be proved to have been definitely drunk until 1840, his failure to make any kind of success of his life, contrasting with his own high expectations, must have been a source of anxiety.

Charlotte's principal anxiety was herself. The letters to Ellen Nussey, the fragmentary and rambling journal she wrote at Roe Head and incoherent scraps of poetry all reveal a morbid preoccupation with her own sinfulness. In particular Charlotte appears to have been worried by her evil thoughts, being too ready to believe that this was a sure sign that she was doomed to damnation. These Calvinist fears have been incorrectly blamed upon Miss Branwell; we do not know where Charlotte read Calvinist doctrines, although Cowper may have been an influence, and even Ellen Nussey may have contributed to her fears.[6]

It is not clear exactly what Charlotte's evil thoughts were. Religious doubts and discontent with her lot were probably combined with sexual feelings normal in adolescence but about which Charlotte was naturally reticent. What is clear is that the world of Angria with its amorous, impious, discontented heroes and heroines, while initially a form of escape from drab reality, became part of Charlotte's secret fears for her own sinfulness. Not only the content of the Angrian stories, but the very fact that Angrian visions could be conjured up without thinking was a reason for worry. The stories begin to have a more realistic and less amoral tone, and in her verse, much of which is incoherent, Charlotte again and again refers to the hold her visions have over her, and the guilt they brought with them.

> Again I find myself alone, and ever
> The same voice like an oracle begins
> Its vague and mystic strain, forgetting never
> Reproaches for a hundred hidden sins,
> And setting mournful penances in sight,
> Terrors and tears for many a watchful night.[7]

In her prose stories of the period at Roe Head Charlotte may be partly drawing on her own preoccupations in bringing Angria into a more realistic frame, and, though the stories still lack the coherence, realism and power of the adult novels they do show a marked improvement on the earlier juvenilia. *Mina Laury* (January 1838) and *Henry Hastings* February–March 1839) both have a governess heroine, although, as Charlotte – unlike Mina – did not have an aristocratic lover, it is probably a mistake to read too much into the description of Elizabeth Hasting's drunken brother Henry; this need not be a reflection of Charlotte's feelings for Branwell. Charlotte's final juvenile work *Ashworth* (1839–41) is principally notable for the marked change towards realism.

Earlier stories, like *Julia* (1837) and *Caroline Vernon* (1839), are still recognisably Angrian, with the political struggle between Zamorna and Northangerland and their rivalry over various mistresses being the principal point of interest. When Charlotte went to Roe Head in 1835 Branwell, with time on his hands, had plunged Angria into war. Northangerland had led a rebellion, Zamorna had been cast into exile and Mary Percy had died of a broken heart. Later she was rather mysteriously revived by Charlotte, and Zamorna recovered his kingdom after a series of battles culminating with the siege and battle of Evesham on 30 June 1837. With this battle the history of

Angria comes to an end, subsequent stories referring to the past as in *Four Years Ago* (21 July 1837) or the future, as in *Stancliffe's Hotel*, where Zamorna City has a distinctly Yorkshire air and there is some crude satire against Methodism as there is in *Julia*.

Owing to the difficulty of dating Charlotte's letters it is hard to know how much Charlotte wrote at Roe Head and how much at home. The question of Branwell's influence in dictating events and ideas is therefore difficult to decide, but it would seem that, although Charlotte wrote in the holidays, and although Branwell dictated the framework of events in Angria, Charlotte was at this period sufficiently independent of her brother's influences to decide the pattern of her own stories.

Charlotte's first term as teacher at Roe Head started, oddly by modern standards, on 29 July 1835. There was quite a long break at Christmas since on 4 January 1838 Charlotte said that term did not start until 30 January. Again in 1838, if we accept the Chitham chronology, Charlotte refers to Easter holidays, although she complains that she had to go back to Dewsbury Moor during them as a result of the death of Miss Wooler's father. In 1836 Charlotte says that 17 June will mark the beginning of vacation, although in 1838 Charlotte was at home in June owing to ill health. As Branwell was in Bradford from May 1838, Charlotte and he were only together at home during the school holidays which would seem on this evidence to have been from Christmas to the end of January, a short break at Easter, and mid June to the end of July.[8]

These dates seem to involve long terms, and it is no wonder that Charlotte twice says to Ellen Nussey that her life involves nothing but the monotony of 'teach, teach, teach'. In one of these letters she complains about long hours. These cannot have allowed much time for writing, and it is therefore not surprising that, while Charlotte wrote poetry and scraps of prose at school, her major stories, *The Return of Zamorna*, *Julia*, *Mina Laury*, *Stancliffe's Hotel* and *The Duke of Zamorna* were written during the holidays, and *Henry Hastings*, *Caroline Vernon* and *Ashworth* were composed after Charlotte had left. In late 1836 Charlotte wonders if Branwell has killed the duchess,[9] but elsewhere we do not have any suggestion that she was influenced or inspired by his presence, and the absence of long prose stories at Roe Head is probably due to lack of time and privacy, a factor which does much to explain the incoherence of what was written during this period.

Another inhibiting factor in Charlotte's writing may have been the advice that she received from the poet Southey. On 29 December 1836 Charlotte wrote a letter to Southey which has not survived. Southey replied belatedly in March 1837 with courteous discouragement, Charlotte thanked him on 16 March, and Southey wrote again (on 22 March) a polite letter commending Charlotte for her good sense in following his advice. It is customary to compare the tact of Charlotte which prompted Southey's courtesy with Branwell's injudicious letter of January 1837 – following his failure to obtain a reply to his letters to *Blackwood's Magazine* – to Wordsworth.[10] In fact the correspondence with Southey does not really show Charlotte in a particularly good light. Southey, bowed down by private grief, and perhaps aware that – though Poet Laureate – his poetic inspiration had long deserted him, counselled her against literature as a profession, saying it was not for women. He called her first letter flighty and thought she wrote under a pseudonym. Clearly Charlotte had tried to unburden her guilt at the way in which poetic inspiration seized her. In her second letter she said that she had 'endeavoured not only attentively to observe all the duties a woman ought to fulfil but to feel deeply interested in them'. This was her father's advice now echoed by Southey. On receiving the second letter Charlotte wrote on the envelope that she was going to keep Southey's advice for ever. Fortunately she did nothing of the kind.

Charlotte had the opportunity to take Southey's advice in 1839 when she received two proposals of marriage. The time was ripe for such a proposal. After a difficult final year as a teacher which had involved a quarrel over Anne's health with Miss Wooler at the end of 1837, and some illness of her own which caused her to be at home in June 1838, she probably returned briefly to the school – now moved to Dewsbury Moor, an unhealthy spot – before leaving finally at the end of the year. On 20 January 1839 she refused an invitation to Ellen Nussey's on the grounds that she had just taken 'a solemn and formal leave' of her acquaintances in the area. In January 1839 Emily was presumably at Law Hill, Branwell at Bradford, and Charlotte and Anne at home, looking out for posts as governesses in private families.

Henry Nussey proposed marriage in March 1839. He must have met Charlotte on her visits to Ellen from Roe Head, although he was at the time of the proposal in Donnington near Chichester. His diary records that he decided to write to Charlotte on the day that he had been refused by his former vicar's daughter, Mary Lutwidge.[11] Henry met this refusal and Charlotte's prompt negative reply with pious equanimity. It was not until six years later that he married Emily Prescott, and Charlotte expressed surprise that he had married before another of Ellen Nussey's brothers, George, whose unsuccessful courtship of Amelia Ringrose strikes a rather bizarre note in Charlotte's correspondence with Ellen.

We could probably guess that Henry was something of a cold fish even if we did not have his sanctimonious diary. Although he did become vicar of Hathersage near Sheffield, where Charlotte and Ellen went to stay, neither his marriage nor his career was successful and he died abroad in obscure circumstances. Nevertheless it is not wholly wrong to connect Henry Nussey with the more heroic St John Rivers. Like St John Rivers Henry Nussey appears to have been a Calvinist Evangelical, thought of being a missionary, offered marriage without love, and his sister was dear to Charlotte in the same way as Jane Eyre likes the Rivers sisters. Moveover Hathersage, which Charlotte visited shortly before starting *Jane Eyre*, is not unlike Moor End; though now a suburb of Sheffield it is close to some impressive moorland scenery. Finally, although Jane's situation, fleeing from Rochester's adulterous proposals, is very unlike that of Charlotte Brontë in 1839, she was like Jane both in turmoil after a difficult emotional year and without any obvious prospects for the future.

There are of course obvious dangers in associating Henry Nussey with St John Rivers. Mr Collins in *Pride and Prejudice* seems a more accurate fictional analogue, and this is not just because Henry Nussey proposed to a girl called Charlotte so rapidly after being refused. The high heroic calling of St John Rivers corresponds with nothing in Henry Nussey's life. Yet Charlotte must have remembered her first proposal with some kind of respect, as most girls do. Henry Nussey was no Zamorna, and appears to have lacked the faintest spark of Rochester's charm, or Paul Emanuel's personality. Yet Charlotte's letter to him is a model of gentle tact as is her letter to Ellen.

Charlotte's second proposal occurred after her first and not very successful experiences as a governess in a private family. She related the proposal of Mr Pryce, the friend of one of her father's curates, Mr Hodgson, in a lighthearted letter of 4 August 1839 to Ellen Nussey. It is difficult to take seriously Charlotte's statements in this letter that she was bound to be an old maid. Like Charlotte's father and her eventual husband Mr Pryce was an Irishman, and Charlotte was attracted by his liveliness and wit, although disturbed by his

Hibernian frivolity. Mr Pryce seems to have been very unlike Henry Nussey, but before Charlotte and before anyone could get to know him, he disappears from the scene, dying of consumption before 24 January 1840.[12]

Before meeting Mr Pryce Charlotte had her first taste of life as a governess in the family of Mr Sidgwick, a rich mill owner, who lived at Stonegappe near Skipton. Charlotte seems to have spent less than two months in this position, since we find her writing a second letter from the Sidgwicks to Emily on 8 June 1839 and telling Ellen Nussey she had left her position a week before 26 July 1839. Some of her time was spent at the house of Mrs Sidgwick's father, Swarcliffe, between Harrogate and Ripon. Near this house was another house, Norton Conyers, later to be brought by Mr Sidgwick's brother. This house carried with it a legend of a madwoman shut in an attic, although we have only the testimony of Ellen Nussey that Charlotte could have used this story as a basis for *Jane Eyre*.[13]

On the other hand Charlotte's dislike of her employer's patronising attitude would seem clearly to have contributed to her feelings about the position of governesses and teachers which play an important part in all of her novels. Unlike Jane Eyre and Lucy Snowe, Charlote Brontë was not venturing into a completely alien world when she went to the Sidgwicks. Neither Stonegappe nor Swarcliffe were all that far from Haworth, Mrs Sidgwick's sister was the wife of the rector of Keighley, and Miss Wooler's brother-in-law, the Reverend Edward Carter, was the curate in charge of Lothersdale, the village near Swarcliffe. Mr Carter had previously been curate of Mirfield, the village near Blake Hall, where Anne Brontë obtained her first post as a governess on 8 April 1839. Here she probably lasted until the Christmas holidays, although she did not find her charges congenial. Unlike the Bloomfields of Wellwood House, unkown and unsympathetic to Agnes Grey, the Inghams should have been, and probably were more friendly as they were related to Ellen Nussey, and the Carter connection, valuable in itself, also provided a means of communication with Charlotte.

There are clearly dangers in looking for too close parallels between the Brontës' own experiences as governesses and the adventures of the heroines of their novels. Agnes Grey and Lucy Snowe after a time, and Jane Eyre almost immediately were successful in their profession. It is doubtful if either Charlotte or Anne achieved similar success with any of their charges, although Anne was to establish in surprising and difficult circumstances, quite unlike those recorded in *Agnes Grey*, some kind of rapport with the daughters of her next employers, the Robinsons of Thorp Green. For Charlotte's first experiences as a governess we have not only the testimony of her novels – wishful thinking though this may be – and her letters with their harsh complaints about the children being riotous, perverse and unmanageable cubs, and Mrs Sidgwick not knowing her, or addressing her harshly or lacking every fine feeling, but also independent testimony from the Benson family, related to the Sidgwicks, and famous in literature and the Church.[14] Admittedly the Bensons were themselves an odd family and their connection with the Sidgwicks was not all that close, but the statement that Charlotte had no gift for the management of children and was in a very morbid condition the whole time has the ring of truth about it.

Mrs Gaskell reports a story that one of the Sidgwick boys said that he loved Miss Brontë and that his mother indignantly rebuked him for presuming to love the governess.[15] This story may have been exaggerated in the telling, but in a way it sums up Charlotte's hunger for love, and resentment and rage that her humble position did not qualify her even for recognition as a human being. These sentiments of the period when Charlotte was a governess were later to find powerful voice in the novels, especially *Villette*, but they were to be sharpened severely during the next five difficult years.

5
Belgium

A modern critic of Emily Brontë, anxious to show that the Brontës were not all that cut off from the world around them, has tried to dispel the legend that Haworth was a remote place by pointing out the number of times the sisters visited such industrial towns as Keighley, Bradford and Leeds.[1] The evidence of Mrs Gaskell, Charlotte and Branwell suggests that there is some truth behind the myth of Haworth's remoteness, and Charlotte's visits to the world outside were not all that frequent.[2] Many of these visits took place between the years 1841 and 1843, but in 1839, at the same time as she was recounting and rebuffing the proposals of Mr Pryce, Charlotte shows the difficulty she had in travelling.

Ellen Nussey and Charlotte wished to go to the seaside in the summer of 1839. Charlotte's aunt and father raised all kinds of objections. Expense can hardly have been one of these, as a rival proposal from Mr Brontë and Miss Branwell to go to Liverpool was mooted. Perhaps Mr Brontë, who was later to object to Mr Nicholls, still feared the influence of Henry Nussey, although in the latter part of 1839 Henry seemed virtually engaged to another lady. This engagement came to nothing, possibly because there was some sort of financial crisis in the Nussey family, tactfully alluded to by Charlotte in a letter to Ellen of December 1839.[3]

Charlotte desperately wrestled with the timetables of coaches, but Mr Brontë objected to this mode of transport. In the end Ellen Nussey took the bull by the horns and arrived in a carriage to sweep Charlotte off, much to the admiration of Branwell who seemed to be at home in September 1839. Charlotte and Ellen travelled some of the distance by rail, the Leeds–York railway line having already been opened, and then by an open carriage to the house of Mr and Mrs Hudson at Easton near Bridlington, then known as Burlington. Easton was some two miles inland from Bridlington, in the direction of Burton Agnes, where Henry Nussey had been curate. Henry would seem to have been responsible for the arrangements of the trip, and it may have been partly his idea that Charlotte and Ellen stayed with the Hudsons instead of undergoing the danger and expense of taking lodgings at Bridlington. Eventually, after a month at the Hudsons' Charlotte and Ellen were allowed to stay a week at Bridlington, although even here the Hudsons visited them every day and helped eke out their modest budget with gifts of food. Most modern readers of the Brontës have less sheltered lives; they are unlikely to find a journey across Yorkshire so difficult, so dangerous or so demanding.

Nor so exciting. Charlotte's letter on her return, dated 24 October is full of pleasant recollections of the sea and of the stay with the Hudsons at Easton. She is equally enthusiastic in a letter of 28 October to Henry Nussey, congratulating him prematurely on his engagement. Ellen Nussey, no doubt pleased with her part in this adventure, may have exaggerated its importance and is probably responsible for the identification of Bridlington with Bretton and of Paulina Hume with Fanny Whipp, the niece of the Hudsons. There seems little to support either identification beyond the casual identity of the initials in the case of Bretton and the fact that Fanny Whipp is one of the few children of whom Charlotte ever spoke kindly. Charlotte did return to Bridlington after Anne Brontë's death at Scarborough some fifteen miles further north; but before the writing of *Villette* – a novel in which the sea plays a large part – she went not to Bridlington, but to Filey which lies half-way between Scarborough and Bridlington.

It would be wrong, however, entirely to eliminate the visit to Bridlington as a source of inspiration for Charlotte's novels in which heroines (or hero in the case of Crimsworth) escape from a period of confinement where they feel their energies and talents stunted. Though Charlotte had been away from home at Mrs Sidgwick's and Miss Wooler's this was the first time she had been really mistress of her own life. She returned home and remained there for fourteen months, although making some efforts to find a post as governess. She expressed her hatred for such a post on more than one occasion. Branwell went as a tutor to Mr Posthlewaite in Broughton for the first six months of 1840, and Anne went to the Robinsons in May or August 1840, but the family was more united than for some time before.

Surprisingly Charlotte did not use this increased leisure or the companionship of her brother and sisters to do much writing. She finished *Caroline Vernon* after returning from Bridlington, and her next story, *Ashworth*, with a realistic setting, would seem to mark a distinct change of emphasis. Written mainly in 1840, though probably revised in 1841, *Ashworth* begins with a biography of Alexander Ashworth, originally called Alexander Percy, and in many other ways related to Northangerland, except that London rather than Verdopolis is the scene of his dissipation and Yorkshire rather than Angria the place of his retreat. On the other hand Charlotte insists that Alexander is not going to be the hero of her tale, this role being given to Algernon West, and she does introduce a scene at a girls' school which is clearly much more in line with the realities of her life than her fantasies. This scene is also much closer to the world of her published novels, in particular to that of *The Professor*, as is the presence of Ashworth's two sons Edward and William, who do not seem very distant from Edward and William Crimsworth.[4]

Ashworth stands half-way between the juvenilia and *The Professor*. Charlotte may have written stories between *Ashworth* and *The Professor*, but not preserved them when she went to Belgium. The preface to *The Professor* talks of 'many a rude effort, destroyed as soon as composed'. It is odd that the only two surviving poems which can be definitely dated to 1840 and 1841 are the Valentine for Mr Weightman and a patriotic poem about the Peninsular War, written when she was a governess at Upperwood House, Rawdon with the Whites. This was later adapted to Britain's Indian campaigns when the poems were published.[5] This meagre poetic output when Charlotte had leisure to write is a great contrast to the outpourings at Roe Head when Charlotte complained that she was worked off her feet.

It may be that Charlotte found it difficult to write because she lacked the inspiration of Angria and of Branwell. Her so-called 'Farewell to Angria' written in 1839, appeared to have been more sincere than other efforts to escape from 'the burning clime where we have sojourned too long'.[6] Branwell had not prospered as an artist at Bradford; his letter to John Brown on his departure for Broughton is definite proof of drunkenness, although there is also an element of bravado in his claims, and there is a vague oral tradition that his dismissal from the Postlethwaites' was due to a drunken debauch.[7] Nevertheless Charlotte could still have hopes for Branwell as she made his shirts and stitched his collars before his departure, talking of 'his variable nature and strong turn for active life'.[8] Branwell's main literary endeavour at this time was a translation of the Odes of Horace, an impressive performance from which Charlotte, without Latin, was necessarily excluded. This translation brought him into contact with Hartley Coleridge, to whom Charlotte sent the first chapters of *Ashworth* in the late summer of 1840. Branwell also wrote to Coleridge, and this shared correspondence might suggest that brother and sister were still in some way co-operating. Coleridge would seem to have replied discouragingly, and Charlotte's reply to him refers sensibly if nostalgically on the one hand to the delights of creating a world out of one's own brain and on the other to her own lack of success in having as the leading characters of her story people who were not 'likely to make an impression upon the heart of any Editor in Christendom'.[9]

Love rather than literature appears to have been Charlotte's main interest in 1840 and 1841. After her two proposals in 1839 Charlotte herself attracted less attention, although she did continue a staid correspondence with Henry Nussey. For a long time Charlotte seems to have been hopeful that Ellen Nussey would marry a neighbouring curate, called Mr Vincent, but he never seems to have got very far in his proposals. Reading between the lines of Charlotte's coy references to Mary Taylor, and in certain cases under the lines with which Ellen Nussey has censored these references, it seems that in 1840 Charlotte thought there was the possibility of a love-affair between Mary and Branwell.[10] Later in 1843 Charlotte seemed to think Ellen might be going to marry one of Mary's two brothers.

Charlotte may have imagined these affairs. The rest of her correspondence is full of the flirtations of the Reverend William Weightman who had come to Haworth as Mr Brontë's curate in August 1839 and remained there until his death in September 1842. Charlotte seemed to think that all who met him would be smitten by his charms, and it is difficult to avoid the impression that she, as well as Ellen Nussey, Sarah Sugden, Caroline Dury and Agnes Walton, a lady in Mr Weightman's native Westmoreland, was captivated by the dashing young curate who does not seem to have been quite truthful about his movements, professing an examination as an excuse for a long absence in July 1840. There is no reason to accuse Mr Weightman of any lack of sobriety, although he was friendly with Branwell, his father was a brewer and his brother, another clergyman, was convicted for drunkenness in 1863.[11]

At all events Mr Weightman was very unlike the sober and colourless Mr Weston of *Agnes Grey*. The initial letter of their surnames seems to be all that the two clergymen have in common.

And yet *Agnes Grey* has been seized upon by those anxious to prove that Anne Brontë was in love with William Weightman. There are some sad love-poems written by Anne, and the fact that she was reluctant to publish these poems may support an unfulfilled love-affair. Anne was at an impressionable age, but she was away as a governess for most of the time Weightman was at Haworth, and Charlotte, keenly interested in the tender secrets of both Mr Weightman and of her friends, only once hinted at any possible love-affair, and that in a most oblique way when she wrote of Weightman in January 1842 'He sits opposite Anne at church sighing softly and looking out of the corners of his eyes to win her attention – and Anne is so quiet, her look so downcast – they are a picture'.[12]

This behaviour in church is not like that of Mr Weston, and, although we do hear one story of Mr Weightman going to the bedside of a girl thought to be dying which reminds us of Mr Weston's kindness to the poor, in points of doctrine Mr Weightman was High Church, and in respect, as well as in certain others, more like the frivolous Mr Hatfield. In April 1840 there was a great debate in Haworth over Church rates with Mr Brontë – aided by Mr Weightman and another curate, Mr Collins – attacking the dissenters. Charlotte did not approve of their intolerant views, but admired their integrity. Before 1840 was out Mr Collins had left his wife, and Charlotte wrote with contempt of his drunken, extravagant and profligate habits. In all Charlotte's novels except *Jane Eyre*, and especially in *Shirley*, the extremes of High and Low Church are treated with equal scorn, and something of Mr Collins enters into the portrait of Mr Malone. Mr Weightman, it seems, was not immortalised.

Charlotte was probably too sensible to dream that his fancy would fall upon her, and her interest in him is unlikely to reflect anything more than the natural curiosity about a lively and attractive young man whose presence must have made Haworth more exciting. Nevertheless, if we were looking for clues from the Brontë novels for what happened in their lives, we could do worse than reflect on Charlotte's experiences being mirrored in part by Anne in *Agnes Grey*. At any rate Charlotte's second employers, the Whites of Upperwood House, Rawdon, do have some links with the Bloomfields of Wellwood House. The Whites were vulgar people whom Charlotte snobbishly despised for looking down on tradesfolk, although their origins were low,[13] in the same way as Agnes despises the upstart Bloomfields. There is the odd fact that Mrs White's maiden name was Robson, the name of Mrs Bloomfield's brother. Charlotte's three charges were a girl of eight and a boy of six, with another baby in the family. The Bloomfield children are of approximately the same age. Charlotte refers to her charges as wild and unruly, though they were better than the Sidgwicks, and she confesses to having a soft spot for the baby.

In fact the Whites do not seem to have been as bad employers as the Bloomfields, and Charlotte, though threatening to give notice in May, lasted until December, claiming to have brought the children under control, and saying that the Whites had made much of her during the last six months of her employment. It was the Whites who were in one way responsible for Charlotte going to Brussels. In the summer holidays Mr Brontë and Miss Branwell had suggested that the three girls set up a school themselves. This prospect is eagerly discussed by Anne and Emily Brontë in their diary papers of 30 July 1841. Charlotte mentioned the proposal in a letter of 19 July 1841. No doubt the idea of running their own establishment, however remote the possibility, helped to keep the Brontës cheerful.

There were however difficulties which became apparent in 1844 when the Brontës tried to turn their dreams into reality. Miss Branwell was willing to make a modest capital contribution, but the venture needed pupils. Miss Wooler, when appealed to for pupils sensibly offered Charlotte a senior post at Dewsbury Moor, but Charlotte after initially accepting her offer turned it down. Dewsbury Moor had not prospered since Charlotte had left it, and Charlotte had no happy memories of it, but the main reason for her reluctance to enter into what was at any rate a going concern was a letter from Mary Taylor who had come home for a short visit from the Continent where she had gone with her sister in the summer of 1841.

It is not difficult to understand the attraction of Europe for Charlotte. From her very early years she had shown an interest in France, with both attraction and repulsion playing their part, as they were later to play a part in the Belgian novels. Charlotte had made progress with her French since she had translated the *Henriade* at the age of fourteen, although in Angrian stories the French had usually been the enemy. In her last two stories both Caroline Vernon and Algernon West had been to Paris. In 1840 we find Charlotte receiving another bale of French books from the Taylors at

Gomersal. This second dispatch contained upwards of forty volumes. Charlotte said they were 'like the rest clever, wicked,
sophisticated and immoral', but she read about half of them pretty
rapidly. We can only guess who were the authors that Charlotte
read at this stage; Paul de Kock, Eugene Sue and George Sand
feature in Hunsden's library. It is not wholly clear when Charlotte
first read Balzac.[14]

The decision to go to Brussels rather than Paris was probably due
to the presence of the Taylors in the former city, although it is
possible that Charlotte may have thought Belgium sounded safer to
her aunt and father. Belgium was also a better place for learning
German. In the event Miss Branwell and Mr Brontë seemed to have
raised little opposition, and after the difficulty of Charlotte travelling with Ellen to Bridlington the journey to distant Brussels with
Emily seems to have been more easily managed. It is true that there
were some slight obstacles. On 17 October Charlotte said to Ellen
that she must not talk of the plan to go to Brussels. On 9 December
she declared that Brussels was still her promised land, but that there
was still the wilderness of time and space to cross. On 20 January
1842 it seemed briefly as if Brussels was to be abandoned in favour of
Lille, and that Charlotte and Emily were to go under the escort of a
Madame Marzials. In the event it was with Mr Brontë, who spent
between two and three weeks in France and Belgium, that Emily
and Charlotte went to Brussels.

Charlotte made two journeys to Belgium and wrote two novels
about her experiences. It is very tempting to draw on these novels
when recounting her adventures in real life – and there are
similarities. Like Lucy Snowe, Charlotte in 1842 saw the sights of
London and stayed at an old-fashioned hotel, the Chapter Coffee
House in Paternoster Row, and the journey between London and
Ostend was as long, and probably as uncomfortable, as that
between London and Boue-Marine. It is possible that in 1843 she
suffered some of the mishaps described in Lucy Snowe's journey to
Villette, although on that occasion she travelled by train and said
she had suffered no accident but a certain amount of anxiety. But in
1842 she had not only the familiar, if not exactly reassuring,
company of Mr Brontë and Emily, but also the presence of Joe and
Mary Taylor, energetic and experienced continental travellers.

The Brontës spent a day in Ostend, and then a day – almost
certainly travelling by coach – *en route* for Brussels. When they
arrived in Brussels they were not like Lucy Snowe, friendless and

alone, but knew where they were going. They spent Monday night in the Hotel d'Hollande and on Tuesday morning – after saying farewell to the Taylors, who were destined for Koekelberg, a village outside Brussels – they presented themselves at the Pensionnat Heger in the Rue d'Isabelle. Mary Taylor, who was not to see the Brontës for another six weeks, said of the parting 'we were of course much preoccupied, and our prospects were gloomy', but Mr Brontë remained in Brussels for a few more days, staying at the house of Mr Jenkins, the Anglican minister in Brussels.

In *The Professor* and *Villette* we are presented with two establishments, a boys' school and a girls' school, situated very close together with a certain amount of joint teaching and formal, if uneasy, co-operation. So it was in real life. Madame Heger had inherited the proprietorship of the girls' school from her aunt, a nun. Monsieur Heger was a teacher at the Athenée Royale, but also gave lessons at his wife's school. The couple had been married since 1836 and had three children with a fourth being born in 1842 and two more subsequently. Though the Hegers had had their share of misfortunes in the past with Madame Heger's father fleeing from France in the revolution of 1789, and Monsieur Heger suffering the loss of his father's fortune and his first wife in a cholera epidemic of 1833, their marriage seems to have been a remarkably happy and successful one. Monsieur Heger was five years younger than his wife, and as rare contemporary photographs show, a handsome man; he was also a man of strong religious convictions.[15]

Pictures of Brussels in the nineteenth century do show that the schools occupied much the same setting as that portrayed in *The Professor* and *Villette*. It is true that much the most extensive treatment of the Belgian schools occurs in *Villette*, written nearly ten years after Charlotte had returned to England, and she must have had a peculiarly retentive memory if she had wanted to recall her Belgian experiences exactly. Nor is there any reason why she should have been so very eager to be exactly autobiographical in certain respects, when as we have seen there are a number of ways in which *The Professor* and *Villette* are not exact records of Charlotte's life.

Still the impressive buildings and pleasant gardens of *Villette* and *The Professor* would seem to have been what Charlotte and Emily would have seen in 1842. Less pleasant and more important are the feelings of isolation, loneliness and claustrophobia which seem to have been something else in common between fact and fiction, although these feelings become more conspicuous in 1843. Not all that many letters to Ellen Nussey survive from 1842. Hostility to Catholicism and to the Belgians is counterbalanced by the enthusiasm Charlotte displayed for her lessons. She was obviously flattered by the invitation for herself and Emily to extend their stay for a second half-year on slightly altered terms with their books and lodging free in return for Charlotte teaching English and Emily music, although she did not like the girls she had met, and complained of some homesickness.[16]

The first famous statement about Monsieur Heger 'a little black ugly being' and his varied moods 'when sometimes he borrows the lineaments of an insane tom-cat, sometimes those of a delirious hyena' but sometimes 'discards these perilous attractions and assumes an air not above 100 degrees removed from mild and gentleman like'[17] clearly reveals a mixture of attraction and repulsion, although at this stage it was as a teacher rather than as a man that Monsieur Heger interested Charlotte. We know a good deal about Monsieur Heger's teaching methods and practice, because we have Charlotte and Emily's French exercises.[18] These show great care and imagination on the part of Monsieur Heger, whose original choice of subjects, careful corrections and ability to make a French lesson also a lesson in history and morality are a model to all teachers. After the dull mechanical lessons at Miss Wooler's, Monsieur Heger must have seemed inspiring, although the severity of his corrections were initially a shock. Initially too there was some difficulty with Emily, but Monsieur Heger was quick to recognise her genius, and Charlotte gave him credit for this.

Unfortunately Emily was forced to go home after nearly a year. This was as a result of Miss Branwell's sudden death, the third in a series of unexpected bereavements which befell the Brontës in the autumn of 1842. Martha Taylor died on 12 October in Belgium of cholera shortly after William Weightman had fallen a victim to the same disease in Yorkshire. Though Martha was not as close to Charlotte as Mary her vivacity and the tragic nature of her death so far from home made a deep impression on Charlotte, and one of the firmest links between fact and fiction in Charlotte's work is the description of Jessie Yorke's death and burial in a foreign graveyard which is introduced movingly, if irrelevantly, into *Shirley*. Miss Branwell's illness was a more protracted one, lasting a fortnight. Branwell said she was fatally ill on 25 October, Charlotte and Emily first heard of her illness on 2 November, but she had died on 29 October. Charlotte and Emily returned home via Antwerp on 5

November carrying with them a letter from Monsieur Heger expressing the hope that the girls would return. Madame Heger wrote subsequently in a similar vein to Charlotte.[19] Miss Branwell, of whom Branwell spoke affectionately and Charlotte respectfully, had left her money to her nieces but not her nephew. The will had been made in 1833 and no insult was intended to Branwell who must, however, have been creating a certain amount of anxiety since he had been dismissed from his post as a railway clerk in April 1842 for negligence.[20]

Charlotte was at home for nearly three months. With the exception of Anne, who only came home from the Robinsons for the Christmas holidays, all the children were at home together. This was the last occasion when the family, although distressed by recent losses, could present a reasonably happy and united front to the world. On her own admission Charlotte was heartbroken the next time she returned in January 1844, and Anne and Branwell's visits to home were short until Branwell's disgrace in June 1845. Charlotte's letters to Ellen Nussey, whom she visited briefly at the end of November 1842 and who visited Haworth in January 1843, speak cheerfully of Branwell and Anne.[21] With the aid of Monsieur Heger's letter it was decided that Charlotte should go to Belgium, Emily remain at home, and then, by what seemed a lucky chance, Branwell was invited to join Anne.

Thus Charlotte had some reason for cheerfulness when she returned, and again we can contrast her departure from her family to an expected welcome in Belgium with Lucy Snowe's lonely journey into the unknown. Once she arrived in Belgium things started to go wrong. The weather was bad; one would have thought that bleak Yorkshire winters would have inured Charlotte to the cold, but in a letter to Ellen in the spring of 1843 she complained of bitterly cold weather. This letter asked whether Ellen had any plans to come to Brussels, and clearly Charlotte was lonely. Mary Taylor was away in Germany, the Jenkins had found it difficult to make friends with the Brontës, and in a letter of 6 March 1843 Charlotte said that the Dixons, Mary Taylor's cousins, were the only people she could go to, and that they were due to leave soon.[22]

Charlotte and Emily had forged some kind of link with the Wheelwrights, an English family who had sent their daughters to the Pensionnat Heger, but though the Wheelwrights remembered Charlotte well, and they renewed their acquaintance when Charlotte was famous, Laetitia, the eldest Wheelwright, was only fourteen in Belgium, and Charlotte expressly distinguishes them from the Dixons as acquaintances rather than friends.[23] It is possible that Laetitia, known in her youth in Belgium and revisited as a young woman in London while Charlotte was composing *Villette*, may have partly inspired Charlotte to write about Polly Hume, known in Britain and seen again in Belgium, although Dr Wheelwright, happliy married with many children, but rather poor, is not all that like Mr Hume, the Comte de Basompierre. The Wheelwrights did, however, live in the same quarter of Belgium and, like the de Basompierres, left Brussels during the long vacation, although in their case for good.

Before this time Charlotte had complained of isolation. She was now a full teacher but did not like the other assistant teachers. They may have been models for some minor characters in *The Professor*, *Villette* and even *Shirley*, and like these characters limited and unfriendly, separated from Charlotte by religion, nationality character and intellectual attainments. Charlotte speaks ill of Mademoiselles Blanche, Haussé and Sophie in a letter to Emily of 29 May, after saying to Ellen Nussey in a letter of 6 March 1843 that Monsieur and Madame Heger were 'the only two persons in the house for whom I really experience regard and esteem'. In the long vacation of August and September Charlotte's letters do reveal the loneliness of Lucy Snowe in *Villette*, and the visit to the confessional in that novel is certainly based on life.[24]

Loneliness rather than love is Lucy Snowe's real trouble, and it may have been Charlotte's. Nevertheless the problem of Monsieur Heger – around which, like the most delicate Victorian biographer, we have been gingerly skirting – must be faced. The evidence for Charlotte's feelings for Monsieur Heger comes from her letters to her friends and family, her own letters to Monsieur Heger after her return, her novels and her poetry. Victorian biographers only had the first and third sets of evidence; the letters, almost certainly not complete, were only discovered in 1914, and the poetry, interesting but uncertain testimony, is only now being properly edited. Even with the letters, the only material with which we are concerned in this chapter, it is clear that something odd and unhappy was happening in 1843, and even with all the evidence it is not quite clear what was happening. Delicacy and decorum probably prevented the chief parties in the affair, Charlotte, Monsieur Heger and his wife, from revealing their feelings to each other, even if they knew them themselves.

Charlotte spoke highly of both Hegers on 6 March. Monsieur

Heger had taken her to the carnival and was having private English lessons with her in the company of his brother-in-law. In April she wrote rather a peculiar letter to Ellen referring to rumours that she was getting married on the Continent. Here she stated that Monsieur Heger was the only man she saw and that seldom. On 1 May, writing to Branwell, she spoke more coolly about Madame Heger, and declared she rarely spoke to Monsieur, although he had been kind to her and loaded her with books. By 29 May there seemed a definite breach with both Hegers, and it would appear that this was largely due to the influence of Madame Heger. There is then no mention of the Hegers until 14 October when Charlotte says in a letter to Ellen that she tried to hand in her resignation, but that Monsieur Heger had prevented her. On the next day she wrote in her atlas that there was 'only one person in this house worthy of being liked – also another, who seems a rosy sugar plum, but I know her to be coloured chalk'.[25]

Eventually Charlotte decided to return, announcing her decision in a letter to Emily on 19 December 1843. In a letter to Ellen Nussey of 15 November she complained that Madame Heger never came near her. On that day Madame gave birth to a baby, a fact unmentioned by Charlotte. Monsieur Heger continued to correct her French compositions throughout the year; some of these show bitterness as well as brilliance.[26] In an unpublished letter to Mary Dixon of 16 October, Charlotte, as well as complaining of loneliness, said that Mary Taylor had invited her to Germany to share her lessons there, but that she had thought of staying till the spring.[27] It is possible that Mary Taylor may have received more confidences than Ellen Nussey, who had her own troubles at this time with the illness of her brother George. Charlotte eventually left Belgium on New Year's Day 1844.

From the above account it is clear that Madame Heger did not behave like Madame Beck or Mademoiselle Reuter, and did not deserve to be portrayed as such. She may have felt that Charlotte was preoccupied in an unhealthy way with her husband, and tried to keep the pair apart. She may have resorted to the spying of which Charlotte accuses both her and her fictional counterparts. Monsieur Heger seems to have behaved well, continuing to teach Charlotte, urging her to stay and giving her a leaving present. He is unlikely to have taken his wife's fears, if she had any, or Charlotte's hopes, if she had any, very seriously. Most of the trouble was in Charlotte's mind, and most of it surfaced only when she returned to England.

6
Author

Charlotte arrived home on 3 January 1844. The journey, about which we hear nothing in fiction, must have been a dispiriting one, but she would have found all the family at home. Ellen Nussey was away in Chichester with her brother, and Mr Brontë's sight was failing. The winter was a harsh one with snow on the ground at the end of February. Anne and Branwell left for the Robinsons' before 23 January, and Charlotte thought they were doing well. Plans for the school took some time in maturing and when matured produced no very satisfactory results. In March Charlotte visited Ellen in Yorkshire, Mary Taylor returned in April, and Ellen visited Haworth at the beginning of July. We have a hitherto unpublished diary of Ellen Nussey's for this year, a scrappy and unsatisfactory document, but one that confirms these comings and goings. Ellen was at Haworth from 1 to 22 July. On 8 July she was at Ponden Hall, where there was plenty of fun and fatigue, on 16 July she walked to a bridge, and on 21 July she attended the Haworth School festival. When Ellen arrived back she commented that home looked almost a paradise. There are two cryptic references to 'High Water' in this diary which scholars are welcome to seize upon as palindromes of Wuthering Heights or Wildfell Hall, or alternatives to Hell, but which probably refer to the weather or the plumbing.[1]

So much for the surface. On 24 July Charlotte wrote to Monsieur Heger in Brussels, beginning with the statement that it was not her turn to write to him. Clearly letters, not preserved, had passed between the couple before this one. Indeed in this letter Charlotte declares that she 'once wrote a letter that was less than reasonable because sorrow was at her heart'.[2] Probably she had written more than one such letter. The letter of 24 July makes painful reading in English and in French. The references to the hard work Monsieur Heger had to undergo and the compliments to Madame Heger strike a false note. The statement about plans to start a school is more sincere. Interestingly Charlotte refers to her ideas of a literary career. Distressingly she refers to the approval of Southey and

Coleridge. Her weakness of sight provides a convenient excuse for not writing too much.

Charlotte's literary activity during the years 1842–5 is obscure. No juvenile manuscripts survive from these years, but she may have destroyed some. She may have taken some such manuscripts over to Belgium. Monsieur Heger, as well as correcting her French prose, may have led her to correct her English prose and verse, and certainly the prose and verse improves after the stay in Brussels. His sage advice that even genius needed constant correction applies to all writers, but had particular application to Charlotte Brontë. Unfortunately it is as difficult to know when Charlotte took his advice as it is difficult to know when Charlotte recognised that her admiration for this advice was not entirely rational. Nevertheless Monsieur Heger deserves more praise for driving Charlotte's novels in the right direction than he deserves for being the inspiration for these novels.[3]

The only poems that we know to be written in Belgium are two translations from the French dated February and March 1843. These poems are written in a German notebook, one of these being the original version of the poem that is reproduced in *The Professor*. The poem 'Parting' though written in 1838, was copied in 1843 at Brussels before being copied again for publication. 'Life' was written in 1839 and also copied at Brussels. The same is probably true of several other published poems, although 'If thou be in a lonely place' was not copied until 30 August 1845. Two long poems, 'Frances' and 'Gilbert', which appear in the German notebook, were probably written in Belgium or when Charlotte returned home, and two poems with a distinctly autobiographical flavour, 'He saw my heart's woe, discerned my heart's anguish' and 'At first I did attention give', seem to belong to the unhappy period when Charlotte was at home, pining for Monsieur Heger.[4]

It is obviously dangerous to read too much autobiography into Charlotte's poetry. We might assume that Charlotte's hatred of the Catholicism she saw in Belgium was reflected in 'Apostasy', but this poem was originally written in 1837. It is tempting to think of Charlotte writing to Monsieur Heger in the poem entitled 'The Letter', but this is another early poem. The sad lines in 'Frances',

> Unloved – I love; unwept I weep
> Grief I restrain – hope I repress
> Vain is this anguish – fixed and deep
> Vainer desires and dreams of bliss.[5]

are almost identical with the first lines of a poem called 'Reason' written as early as 1836. We find it, however, difficult to avoid thinking of Monsieur Heger when reading some of the lines in 'Frances' which describes how a girl is left forlorn by her lover. It is true that this lover 'went a roving / To sunny climes beyond the sea', but references to his change of feeling, and failure to send word or token of friendship do seem to reflect Charlotte's own bitterness.

'Gilbert' is more dramatic. It tells of how a prosperous married man is visited by the apparition of a woman whom he has abandoned. He sees her drowned, and then after ten years the ghost returns, driving Gilbert to suicide. Now Monsieur Heger had not of course made any promises to Charlotte, nor did she drown herself, but there is a strong emphasis on desertion in both 'Frances' and 'Gilbert', just as there is a strong emphasis on loneliness in the poems written at Roe Head, and Charlotte must have felt deserted in the period after she left Belgium since she said to Ellen Nussey that the decision to return to Belgium resulted in a total withdrawal for more than two years of happiness and peace of mind.

Two poems that seem to have definite autobiographical links are 'He saw my heart's woe, discerned my soul's anguish' and 'At first I did attention give'. These may have been written after these years of agony were over; neither provide accurate biographical information. When Charlotte says in the former poem 'once a year he heard a whisper low and dreary', the tone reminds us of her letters to Monsieur Heger, but she sent these more frequently. In the latter poem, where respect and affection change into a lawless love thwarted by a rival, Charlotte, if she is talking about herself, envisages an adulterous relationship which clearly did not take place. She later used this poem with a change of sex to express Rochester's feelings as he contemplated a bigamous marriage with Jane Eyre.

Charlotte may have felt that she would like Madame Heger to die and Monsieur Heger to have married her, but she must have known that neither of these events was very likely. In the two years that followed her departure from Belgium it seems that imprudence on her part and negligence on Monsieur Heger's destroyed even the bond of friendship which was all that Charlotte could claim from her love. The letters we have do not seem rash enough to explain Monsieur Heger's silence, but there were others, and it is not clear how far Madame Heger intervened. According to Laetitia Wheelwright, at one stage Charlotte was directing her letters to the boys' school on Monsieur Heger's instructions.[6] He wrote to Charlotte in April, Charlotte wrote in May a letter that has not been found, wrote again in July, then in October sent a letter via Joe Taylor to be delivered in person. Charlotte wrote a more neurotic letter on 8 January 1845, and then again on 18 May another letter that has not survived.

This would seem to have wrung a reply as in her next letter, dated 18 November 1845, Charlotte refers to the six month's ration which Monsieur Heger had imposed. She asks if she may write again in May 1846, but Monsieur Heger may not have replied, or replied so discouragingly that Charlotte gave up the unequal struggle.

On the last letter Monsieur Heger scribbled unromantically the address of a shoemaker, and it is difficult when reading Charlotte's desperate pleas for help not to feel irritation with the man who had made her so unhappy. We do not have all the correspondence, but what we do have suggests that the policy of sternness and neglect which Monsieur Heger seems to have adopted towards the end of the correspondence only made Charlotte more unhappy, as the early letters are more cheerful. Perhaps Madame Heger was partly to blame. Nor can posterity entirely blame the Hegers for their unkindness, since eventually Charlotte was able to transform her unhappiness into great art.

The Professor, though not a great novel, is a novel full of Charlotte's recent experiences as a teacher in Belgium. We do not know when Charlotte began work on *The Professor*. The novel as we have it was revised after *Shirley*, and there are various fragments in which Charlotte tried to recast the opening chapters. It is possible that the novel which Charlotte had almost completed when she wrote to Aylott and Jones on 6 April 1846 was shorter than the one we now have. It may not have included the slightly incongruous Yorkshire chapters, although these explore the familiar subject of the rivalry of two brothers. Even as it stands *The Professor* is not a long novel, and could have been written in the winter of 1845. Family circumstances make this the most likely date.[7]

By the winter of 1845 the Brontë family was in a bad way. When Charlotte returned home in 1844 she remarked that Anne and Branwell were 'wondrously valued' in their situations, but that her father was becoming old and blind. The plan for a school is mentioned in July to Monsieur Heger and at about the same time to Ellen Nussey, but in spite of efforts by Ellen to distribute circulars by October Charlotte had to confess that no pupils were to be had. The winter of 1844 cannot have been a cheerful one. Ellen Nussey had her own troubles with her brother George, Mary Taylor departed in March 1845 for New Zealand and Charlotte's own health was not good. A letter to Ellen of 24 March 1845 reads drearily.

> I can hardly tell you how time gets on here at Haworth. There is no event whatever to mark its progress – one day resembles another – and all here have lifeless physiognomies – Sunday-baking-day and Saturday are the only ones that bear the slightest distinctive mark – meantime life wears away – I shall soon be 30 – and I have done nothing yet.[8]

The arrival of Mr Nicholls as Mr Brontë's curate in May cannot have excited Charlotte much. She speaks ill of her father's curates in a letter a month later as a self-seeking, vain, empty race.[9] In the same letter Charlotte mentions the return of Anne and Branwell from the Robinsons. Anne terminated her employment at this point, but Branwell went back. From 26 June to 19 July Charlotte stayed with Ellen at Hathersage Vicarage where Henry Nussey, who had at last married, was the incumbent. Mr and Mrs Nussey were away when Charlotte was staying. The visit may have provided some inspiration for *Jane Eyre*.

On her return home Charlotte found Branwell drowning his sorrows since Mr Robinson had dismissed him for 'proceedings bad beyond expression'. We shall probably never know for certain what these proceedings were. The combination of Branwell's vivid imagination on the one hand and Victorian respectability on the other have ensnared many biographers from Mrs Gaskell onwards. It is possible that Branwell merely became disgustingly drunk. There are tactful references to ill health in the letter of Charlotte to Monsieur Heger in October 1844 and in Anne's diary paper of 30 July 1845.[10] In October 1845 Branwell, in a letter to Francis Grundy, said there was a love-affair between him and Mrs Robinson, and embellished this story with additions, some of them demonstrably false, in the remaining three years of his life. It is possible that Branwell imagined the love-affair or invented it in order to conceal some less romantic sin. If the love-affair did exist we do not know how far it went. Mr Robinson appears to have forgiven his wife.[11]

The Brontë sisters would seem to have believed the worst of Mrs Robinson, seen as prime mover in the affair in Mrs Gaskell's account. Mrs Gaskell had to retract this story which she presumably obtained from Charlotte, but her retraction in no way disproves what seems clear, namely that Charlotte and her sisters believed that their brother was engaged in an adulterous affair with a married woman. It is true that Charlotte, though more censorious than her sisters – who in their diary papers record the pious hope that Branwell will do better – is only censorious about Branwell's drunkenness, debts and apathy. She never mentions Mrs Robinson until June 1846, the occasion of Mr Robinson's death, when she expresses a certain amount of doubt in Branwell's veracity, and she was right to doubt the story about Mrs Robinson being debarred from marrying again by a codicil in Mr Robinson's will because no such codicil existed.[12]

Adultery and drunkenness play some part in all the Brontë novels completed in Branwell's lifetime. They are most conspicuous in *The Tenant of Wildfell Hall*, written at a time when Branwell's drunkenness was in its most advanced stage, and by the only sister who had met Mrs Robinson. In *Jane Eyre* Mrs Rochester is both unchaste and intemperate, and Jane flees the temptations offered by Rochester, but Rochester's own sexual laxity is treated relatively generously. In *Wuthering Heights* Hindley is frequently drunk, but not savagely condemned, and it seems almost blasphemous to talk of the love of Catherine and Heathcliff as adulterous, even if, as seems unlikely, adultery takes place. In *Agnes Grey* there are incidental and disapproving mentions of adultery and drunkenness in connection with Sir Thomas Ashby, while in *The Professor* Monsieur Pelet gets drunk on one occasion, and Crimsworth fears for his own virtue if he and the newly married Pelets live under one roof.

Contemporary readers found all this shocking, but modern readers find it hard to see what all the fuss was about, especially when, except in *Wuthering Heights*, the Brontës are anxious to condemn what they describe, although not perhaps strongly enough for Victorian taste. In Charlotte's juvenile stories the author is less prone to condemn drunkenness and sexual misdemeanours than in her mature novels, and perhaps the impact of Branwell's experiences on his sisters' mature novels can be summed up as follows. He had shown them the sordid side of drinking and the unhappiness caused by affairs with married women. This dispelled any lingering traces of Byronic romanticism about such sins, and indeed impelled Anne, as the preface to *The Tenant of Wildfell Hall* makes clear, to paint them in their darkest colours. On the other hand Branwell was their brother, and the sisters – especially Emily –

were likely to be more forgiving than most of their readers. Charlotte adopts a position in her fiction midway between her two sisters, although in her letters she is very harsh to Branwell. Branwell had once been the closest of the family to her, and she had not sought solace in drink for a love-affair that had gone wrong. Mr Brontë's increasing infirmity during the years 1845 and 1846 made Charlotte anxious, and she must have felt that Branwell was hardly helping his family in their hour of need.

In their despair the Brontë sisters had some solace. The story of the publication of their poems is an interesting one. Our principal source is the preface Charlotte wrote to the posthumous second edition of her sisters' works when, in 1850, the kindly and efficient George Smith took over these works from the incompetent Thomas Newby. Clearly Charlotte, still mourning for her sisters, was anxious to show them in as good a light as possible, and, with her own fame assured, she had no need to stress her own part in the publication of the poetry. Nevertheless the correspondence with Aylott and Jones is signed by Currer Bell, and there is every reason to suppose that Charlotte played the leading part in arranging the publication of the poems. Her own account suggests that Emily and Anne would not have dared venture into print without her.[13]

Charlotte says that she came across Emily's poetry by accident in the autumn of 1845, and was more than surprised by the vigour and sincerity of their thought and the wild, melancholy and elevating nature of their music. Emily was annoyed by the discovery, and it took days to reconcile her to the thought that such poetry merited publication. Anne produced her poems, and Charlotte found them too worthy of praise, although – as so often with Anne – the praise is mixed with condescension, as Charlotte describes her younger sister's verses as having 'a sweet sincere pathos of their own'. Charlotte is modest about her own contribution, and this is only natural in a preface to an edition of the works of Ellis and Acton Bell, which included some new poems by Emily and Anne, but nothing by Charlotte. In the printed edition of 1846, however, the poems of Currer Bell, although the worst, are also the first to catch the reader's eye.[14]

On 30 January 1846 Charlotte wrote to Miss Wooler a strange letter, complaining of Branwell's misconduct, making some sensible remarks about the upbringing of boys and girls – very much in the manner of Helen Huntingdon – and saying that the lot of an unmarried woman was not a bad one. Charlotte had rather less than three months before she crossed the spinster's Rubicon of being thirty, and we perhaps need not read too much into this letter to Miss Wooler, very different from the despairing letter to the differently situated Monsieur Heger two and a half months earlier. The letter is, however, interesting because it contains some odd remarks about Emily's handling of the Brontës' small investment in railway shares. 'As long as we regard those we love, and to whom we are closely allied, with profound and never-shaken esteem, it is a small thing that they should vex us occasionally by, what appears to us, unreasonable and headstrong behaviour'.[15]

It is hard for those of us interested in literature to think of the Brontë sisters as amateur stockbrokers, and tempting to see this squabble over investments as masking a more fundamental quarrel over literature. Charlotte's relationship with her two sisters in the two years before their death and her reaction to their death will be discussed in full in the next chapter, but certainly the letter to Miss Wooler proves that the bond between Charlotte and her sisters was, though a close one, also subject to certain stresses. These stresses are likely to have shown themselves in the joint effort of publication as much as in the handling of railway shares. Emily's part in the latter suggests that she is unlikely to have left all the publication in Charlotte's hands. The idea that the discovery of her poetry destroyed all the poetry in Emily, and eventually Emily herself, is a romantic one, but not supported by concrete evidence except for the fact that not much poetry of Emily's survives after 1845. This does not mean she did not write any, and it is probable that she did edit her own poems for the 1846 selection rather than, as has sometimes been supposed, tamely leaving the selection and text in the hands of Charlotte.[16]

Selecting which poems to publish cannot have been an easy task. A modern editor has merely to select the best poems, or perhaps those with most biographical interest. In 1845 the Brontës did not know that their lives would be of interest, and indeed there may have been reasons why they should try and suppress certain poems which revealed their lives too clearly. Nor can it have been easy to select the best as both Gondal and Angria were a part of the background of many poems. In addition, although Emily's poems were clearly the best, it was also the wish of all three sisters that each should be represented in the selection in an equal proportion; presumably each sister selected her own poems. We do not know whether there was any editorial policy about spelling, punctuation

or the elimination of Gondal or Angrian references. Since the
Brontës were paying Aylott and Jones for the privilege of being
published, the form of the poems need not have concerned the
publishers unduly, although they probably in a tactful way elimin-
ated some of the more unruly eccentricities of presentation.[17]

Emily and Anne were still actively engaged in Gondal in 1845,
whereas Charlotte had finished with Angria by 1839. It should
therefore have been easier for Charlotte to prepare her own
selection, although the final choice is not a wholly satisfactory one.
Possibly in an effort to conform with Victorian taste Charlotte
includes long narrative poems and statements of an optimistic
philosophy which seem extremely forced.

> Life, believe, is not a dream
> So dark as sages say;
> Oft a little morning rain
> Foretells a glorious day.[18]

This poem, which had originally been written in 1839, and copied
again in 1843, with its trite cheerfulness contrasts strangely with
Emily's original despair. Perhaps it was included to balance this
despair or the general gloom of the previously discussed 'Gilbert'
and 'Frances'. Some of the other poems which tell a story, albeit
rather an obscure one, are concerned with a man called William,
with whom a woman faces separations and dangers. In 'Apostasy'
the hero is originally called William, but this is changed to Walter in
the final version; in this poem the heroine refuses to renounce her
faith and dies. In 'Regret' the heroine mourns the absence of William
across the sea, but in 'The Wood' and 'The Wife's Will' the lovers are
united. In the latter poem they are united in France – a dangerous
place at the time of the First Consulate as Charlotte comments in a
footnote.[19] In 'The Wood' the lovers seem separated for a time by the
English Channel.

'Never doubt that Fate is keeping / Future good for present ill':[20] so
Charlotte concludes a falsely cheerful poem entitled 'Parting'. These
lines were proved cruelly false in the next three years, and a poem
entitled 'Presentiment' about two sisters talking together in the
winter, during which one of them was to die, was to prove tragically
true. Such poems and others involving separation, such as 'The
Letter', which clearly have an Angrian context are warnings against
the idea that Charlotte could only publish poems about her own

particular concerns in 1845. Nevertheless while we must be careful of too strict an autobiographical interpretation it is not exactly surprising that with Monsieur Heger in her mind Charlotte should choose so many poems involving the separation of lovers, a recurring theme in her novels. Nor is it surprising that such nakedly autobiographical poems as 'At first I did attention give' and 'He saw my heart's woe, discerned my soul's anguish' are excluded; they may not have been written by the time the poems were sent to the printer, but even if they had been written Charlotte could hardly have revealed them to her sisters, let alone to the world. Only when suitably disguised does Monsieur Heger enter into the poetry.

The first and last poems in Charlotte's selection have a religious theme, and may have been written especially for Aylott and Jones, a firm of publishers who specialized in books connected with the Church. Even in these poems love and marriage find a place. Pilate's wife appreciates with conventional orthodoxy the power of Christ, but shows an unconventional lack of loyalty to her husband. The final poem, 'The Missionary' has echoes of St John Rivers as it tells of a devoted servant of the Church abandoning the love of a lady called Helen for the task of converting the heathen in India. This poem is worth reading in connection with the surprising conclusion of *Jane Eyre*.

Charlotte, when she wrote to W. S. Williams in September 1848 on the occasion of Smith Elder and Co. taking over the publication of the poems, is modest about her own contribution. She said that much of it was written in early youth.[21] This is not really true, since of the nineteen poems printed only ten can be definitely proved to have been written before 1840, and most of these were written in 1837. Charlotte was twenty-one in 1837, and this is hardly early youth; moreover some of these poems were revised at a later date. Modern selections of Charlotte's poems usually include for the sake of completeness some much earlier poems. Charlotte also declares in 1848 that she found much of her poetry crude and rhapsodical. It is true that the poems are marred by rhetorical outbursts by characters of whose circumstances we know little, whereas it would seem that Charlotte's gifts lay in the description of her own feelings or in the description of her surroundings. Charlotte wrote two very fine poems on the occasion of her sister's death, some wild poems describing her loneliness at Roe Head and in Brussels or just after, and some technically excellent poems in early youth. For a variety of reasons these could not be included in her final selection.

Making the proper selection and overcoming Emily's objections were not the only difficulties the Brontës faced in getting their poems published: they also had to find a publisher. Charlotte waxes eloquent about this problem.[22] Eventually Chambers of Edinburgh recommended Aylott and Jones, and Charlotte wrote to them on 28 January. Thereafter publication proceeded with commendable briskness. Aylott and Jones immediately agreed to publish the poems at the authors' risk and Charlotte despatched the manuscript on 7 February. On 15 February she wrote anxiously to enquire whether the two parcels had arrived, but on 13 February Aylott and Jones had written with technical advice on the printing. On 3 March Charlotte despatched the sum of £31. 10s., a large contribution from three unemployed ladies, whose father was nearly blind and whose brother was nearly always drunk, as Charlotte announced to Ellen in a letter of the same date. She later had to send an additional £5.

The poems were published at the end of May 1846. Charlotte asked that copies should be sent to a number of periodicals; *The Critic*, *The Athenaeum* and *The Dublin University Review* gave reasonably favourable reviews, but, as with so many of the Brontë ventures, the high hopes the Brontës had entertained ended in ludicrous failure. Only two copies of the poems were sold, and though Mr Aylott of Aylott and Jones tactfully advised against further expenditure on advertising, the Brontës must have been considerably out of pocket.[23]

Fortunately they had something else to fall back upon. Before the poems were printed Charlotte was enquiring (6 April 1846) from Aylott and Jones about three distinct works of fiction which were nearly completed. Aylott and Jones presumably recommended a few publishers; they did not publish fiction, and in the case of their novels the Brontës did not intend to publish at their own expense. The manuscript of *The Professor* is dated 27 June, and on 4 July Charlotte wrote to Henry Colburn asking if she might send the three novels. It would seem that all three Brontës were active with novel writing at the same time as their poems were being prepared for the press. Such activity need not surprise us. All three sisters were continuously at home for the first time since 1835, and although the novels are surprisingly distinct we have some evidence of the three Brontës working together and encouraging each other. The publication of the poems, far from being a distraction, must have acted as a spur, and it is noticeable how each author develops in her novel some of the themes of her poetry. In Charlotte's case we have both in the poems and in *The Professor* lovers called Frances and William, lovers who are separated and united, hostility to Roman Catholicism, feelings of loneliness and illness, some strained soliloquies and tame happy endings. Indeed many of the faults of Charlotte's poetry are there in her first novel, just as much of the strength of *Wuthering Heights* is in Emily's poetry, while Anne's verse and *Agnes Grey* breathe the same note of pious resignation.

The story of *The Professor*'s journeys round various publishers belongs to the next chapter where it is impossible to separate Charlotte's story from that of her sisters. This novel has not received a great deal of critical admiration and probably does not deserve much. The eccentric beginning in Yorkshire, although going back to the Angrian theme of the rivalry of two brothers, may be a late addition from the time when Charlotte tried to revise the novel before embarking on *Villette*. The strongly feminine male narrator may be part of Charlotte's efforts to throw a smokescreen over her exploits in Belgium, the scenery of which she faithfully records. Crimsworth's surprising success with his recalcitrant pupils and his eventual good luck in obtaining a school of his own and a wife suited to his temperament owe a lot to wishful thinking. Those who see the novel as autobiographical ignore these differences; it is these same differences which prevent Charlotte from writing at her best. The love-affair between Crimsworth and Frances is a very tepid one, though it results in a happy marriage. In the world of *Jane Eyre*, which is a very different one from the humdrum existence of Charlotte Brontë and of William Crimsworth, Charlotte was able to give full rein to the passion she felt.

7

Jane Eyre

All of Charlotte Brontë's novels were composed in adverse circumstances. When writing *The Professor* she was heartsick for Monsieur Heger, her two sisters died while she was engaged on *Shirley*, and the years she spent on *Villette* were ones of intense loneliness, marred by ill health. *Jane Eyre* was written at a time when calamity had not yet fallen on her family, and when the wounds left by Brussels were less fresh; but it would be wrong to assume that Charlotte's lot was a happy one when she wrote *Jane Eyre*. She is supposed to have begun writing when taking her father to Manchester for an operation on his eyes.[1] Surprisingly, in view of Mr Brontë's age and the primitive state of medicine at the time, the operation was a complete success, and the spectre of blindness and enforced retirement which must have haunted the sisters eventually retreated, but it would undoubtedly have been a worrying time. Branwell's troubles continued; as well as drunkenness and debauchery the disgrace of debt pursued him: on 13 December 1846 a Sherriff's officer arrived from York demanding payment or arrest. The winter was a savagely cold one.[2]

All these distressing distractions Charlotte faithfully reported to Ellen Nussey who was away from Yorkshire for some of the winter. A visit to Haworth was promised in May, but never materialised. What Charlotte did not report to her dearest friend was another source of disappointment: the apparent failure of her literary ventures. Not only did the poems fail to sell but publisher after publisher turned down the novels. One such rejection occurred when Charlotte was in Manchester; she defiantly began *Jane Eyre*, a novel about triumph over adversity, although not one that reflects the immediate concerns of Charlotte's life.[3]

Charlotte's secrecy about her novel writing, which she maintained until well after the publication of *Jane Eyre*, needs some explanation. Admittedly Ellen Nussey was not a lady interested in literature, and her timid prudery in other matters suggests that she might, like some readers and critics of *Jane Eyre*, have been shocked by what was called coarseness. Moreover Charlotte was used to

74

secrecy. It seems clear that her father knew nothing of *Jane Eyre* until it was published. It would appear that Branwell was also kept in the dark, although he still harboured literary ambitions, writing to Leyland about a possible volume of poems as late as April 1846, and he had some poems published in the local newspapers. Since his sisters had always been writing, and since he was rarely sober, it was presumably not difficult to keep the secret from him.[4]

What would be interesting to find out is how the sisters behaved towards each other during the series of disappointing rejections. At some point *The Professor* was separated from *Agnes Grey* and *Wuthering Heights*, and sent to different publishers. This was probably at some time during the bleak winter of 1846. There are various possible reasons for this decision. One of the publishers who rejected all three novels may have hinted that they might have stood more chance of success if submitted singly or in a pair. A publisher may have seen, not surprisingly, more merit in *Wuthering Heights* than in its two companions, and Charlotte may have decided to remove *The Professor* to aid her sisters. It is possible that *Wuthering Heights* originally existed in a much shorter form and that Emily was advised to extend it, thus rendering *The Professor* superfluous.[5]

All these reasons may have led to a perfectly amicable decision to let *The Professor* go its separate way; but it is possible that the separation may have been less than amicable. Since Emily had created trouble over railway shares and the publication of her poems, it seems quite likely that the publication of her novel would also create difficulty. Since the only account we have of the efforts to publish *Agnes Grey*, *Wuthering Heights* and *The Professor* together comes from Charlotte's preface to the second edition of the two former novels, it is not surprising that no mention of any difficulty occurs in this account. Charlotte was very fond of her two sisters, and the yawning gap left by their death can hardly have increased her willingness to stress any divisions that may have arisen. Vague references to the Brontës working together and a natural tendency to regard the three sisters as one author should be balanced against the considerable differences between the three novelists and their novels. Even when there are similarities between such novels as *Wuthering Heights* and *The Tenant of Wildfell Hall*, these similarities merely point to differences. In the case of the first three novels it would seem that *The Professor* and *Agnes Grey* with their quiet talk of teachers have more in common than the wild notes of *Wuthering*

Heights. On the other hand Anne and Emily, though not totally in accord in the last two years of their life, had worked together on Gondal right up to the writing of *Agnes Grey* and *Wuthering Heights*, and it is not surprising to find them working together over their publication.

The Professor is the only one of the three novels to be set in Belgium. It is possible that a publisher may have seen this as a reason for singling out this novel, or indeed that the three sisters may have agreed upon this point. Alternatively it is just possible that Anne and Emily may have found the disguised presence of Monsieur Heger something of an embarrassment. We do not know and cannot tell how much Charlotte told Emily and Anne about her lawless love for her teacher. A modern family would have made ribald jokes about Charlotte creeping down to meet the postman who might be carrying letters from a lover. The Brontës were not a modern family, and after the sad suffering of Branwell's sins with a married woman they cannot have looked lightly on any correspondence with Monsieur Heger. It is sometimes alleged that Charlotte confided in Emily about her troubles on the evidence of a statement in her last letter to Monsieur Heger that she had ceased to speak about him to her sister.[6] On the contrary this suggests that Charlotte talked to Emily for a time as if he had been only her teacher, but eventually found this too painful. Emily may well have guessed the secret, but shyness, sympathy and some kind of disapproval would have prevented her from taking the issue up with Charlotte. She may have discussed the matter with Anne, but it is at this time that the co-operation between Anne and Emily ceased to be that of people almost like twins. *The Tenant of Wildfell Hall* is not a pale imitation of *Wuthering Heights*, but a dark attack upon it. Anne's poetry is in many ways a refutation of the apparently blasphemous sentiments of Emily. Haworth Parsonage probably saw no open rows in the bitter winters of 1845 and 1846, but plenty of stiff upper lips.

Charlotte's achievement in writing *Jane Eyre*, a brave novel about triumph against adversity, is a remarkable tribute to the resilience of the human heart, and though it is possible to find fault with Charlotte on various scores, nobody can doubt her indomitable courage. Her letters to Ellen Nussey in the winter of 1847, as well as complaining about the weather and about Branwell, describe the stifling boredom of her existence. 'I know life is passing away and I am doing nothing', 'I am now in that unenviable frame of mind – my humour I think is too soon overthrown – too sore – too demonstrative and vehement', 'I'm in danger sometimes of falling into self-weariness', 'I look almost old enough to be your mother – grey – sunk – and withered'.[7]

From this dreary, middle-aged ennui Charlotte was able to create an exciting story with a happy ending about a young woman, who, in spite of cruel restricting disadvantages, wins her way to fulfilment and happiness by the strength of her character. There is, of course, something of Charlotte in Jane; the heroines' loneliness, sense of confinement and strong hatred of injustice are shared by the author. On the other hand certain scenes and characters and episodes in the plot appear to owe more to the fantastic world of Angria than to the drab world of Charlotte Brontë. It is these features of the novel which have received most criticism. The strange coincidences, the unreal atmosphere of the house party at Thornfield and the wild behaviour of Mr Rochester have seemed incredible to readers, both contemporary and modern.

Mr Rochester contains something of Monsieur Heger, something of Zamorna, but also, as we have seen, something of Charlotte herself, and he and his suitability for Jane are better appreciated in this light. Blanche Ingram and her entourage are artificial, but are of course meant to be; here Charlotte is using somewhat crude satire to take revenge on the world she felt had passed her by. The coincidences which recur in all the novels are perhaps harder to excuse. The way in which everybody in the novel seems to know everybody else is a consequence of Charlotte's restricted upbringing among a narrow circle of acquaintances. We would not really expect Miss Temple to know Mr Lloyd, the apothecary at Gateshead, or Mr Rochester to have much knowledge of Mr Brocklehurst. The fortunate device whereby Jane, alone and helpless, collapses outside the door of her long-lost cousins is as improbable as the similar scene in *Villette* where Lucy Snowe is rescued in a faint by her godmother's son. Both heroines are tempted to think that they may have found their husbands, and the other relationship, though clumsily established, does have something of the brother–sister link which is all that Jane wants from St John and Lucy can get from John Graham. It is probably wrong to make any equation between Diana and Mary Rivers, and Emily and Anne Brontë; the fictional heroines are outwardly more spirited and attractive, their relationship is not the same, and, as we have tried to show, there was probably rather less harmony at Haworth Parsonage than at Moor End.

The outrageous rescue by Rochester crying 'Jane' three times when she was about to accept the proposal of St John Rivers has offended many readers. It was apparently based on an incident in real life, but an exact identification is unlikely, and speculation about possible parallels fairly fruitless. It is of course necessary to have some strong reason for Jane to go back to Rochester, since if she had gone back on impulse without supernatural intervention she might well deserve St John's accusations of immorality. There is a strong belief in providence in *Jane Eyre* and in Charlotte's letters, and by a curious coincidence the very good fortune which suddenly befalls Jane after all her troubles now blessed Charlotte in connection with the publication of her first novel.

Charlotte sent *The Professor* to Smith Elder on 15 July 1847; on 2 August she wrote a letter asking whether they had received the parcel. Very soon after this she received a courteously worded refusal, stating that a three-volume novel would meet with careful attention, and providentially she had *Jane Eyre*, almost ready, announcing on 7 August 1847 that she would send a novel in a month's time and in fact dispatching it on 24 August. It is possible that the happy but hasty conclusion of *Jane Eyre* owes something to this chain of circumstances. Charlotte thanks Smith Elder for their help with punctuation and is unlikely to have had the time in August for revision of minutiae. The contract between author and publisher was finally made on 12 September.[8]

The three sisters had adopted the pseudonyms of Currer, Ellis and Acton Bell for their poetry, feeling it wrong, according to Charlotte, to adopt definitely masculine names, but suspecting that female authors were at a disadvantage.[9] They continued this policy with their novels. Smith Elder who had had the manuscripts and numerous letters, including some asking for replies to be addressed to Mr Currer Bell c/o Miss Brontë, had no difficulty in detecting the sex of their correspondent, but kept the secret so well that when the novel came out there was considerable speculation as to the sex of the author, and in late 1848 Lockhart said that it was commonly believed that the Bells were brothers of the weaving fraternity in Lancashire.[10] Reviewers of *Jane Eyre* were generally more perceptive about the sex of the author, although some of their accusations of coarseness make the Brontës' caution in not publishing under their own name very understandable. G. H. Lewes, when considering the novels of George Eliot – equally fatuously confused with a Nonconformist clergyman called Liggins – commented that the reputation of *Jane Eyre* had suffered when it was known to be by a woman.[11]

It was not just their sex that the Brontës wanted to keep from the public eye. They resolutely kept knowledge of their writing from their family and closest friends like Ellen Nussey. Ellen was told by Anne Brontë on 4 January 1848 that they had done nothing (to speak of) since Ellen last wrote. Ellen said later that she had seen Charlotte correcting proofs at Brookroyd which she had visited in September, but had respected Charlotte's privacy. On 3 May Charlotte still denied to Ellen that she had been publishing, and on 26 June said she was not qualified to give any opinion on the latest new novel.[12] This was probably *Jane Eyre*. Eventually the secret had to come out. Charlotte maintained that it was her sisters' wish that their identity should not be revealed, and in view of Emily's reluctance to publish her poems and the autobiographical nature of *Agnes Grey* this is probably true.

Wuthering Heights and *Agnes Grey* had been accepted by Thomas Newby, on terms which were not particularly advantageous, some time before Charlotte completed *Jane Eyre*. It is not certain whether Newby was offered *The Professor*; it is possible that Charlotte may have disagreed with her sisters about the bargain Newby had struck. She contrasted the promptness of Smith Elder with the dilatoriness of Newby, and since the proofs of *Agnes Grey* and *Wuthering Heights* had been sent to Haworth by August it is quite likely that the three novels had parted company as early as the spring of 1847. By the autumn they were keeping pace again with the proofs having to be corrected. Charlotte talks about this in letters of 24 and 29 September, and by 16 October *Jane Eyre* was published some seven weeks after it had first been read by George Smith in the space of a day.[13] Modern authors are lucky if only seven months elapse between the submission of a manuscript and the publication of a book. So much for progress and the resources of modern technology.

Admittedly not all modern authors are likely to have been selected for such special treatment as Charlotte Brontë. W. S. Williams and George Smith deserve great credit for recognising the exciting originality of *Jane Eyre* and were rewarded by its success, for which they may have done some preliminary work, since the favourable reviews followed almost instantly on publication. Letters from Williams to Charlotte seem to prepare her for fame before publication, and in spite of some modest demurrals Charlotte did not seem surprised by the enthusiastic reception of her work. It is just possible that Newby may have heard about Currer Bell's work in advance and timed the publication of the books of Acton Bell and Ellis Bell in December in order to gain favourable publicity, although confusion between the three Bells does not really begin until 1848, and *Wuthering Heights* and *Agnes Grey* were not very favourably received.[14]

It is one of the marks of genius to have no doubt in one's ability and Charlotte's acceptance of her rise to fame was remarkably placid. As good reviews came pouring in, sales increased, and by 10 December Charlotte was thanking Smith Elder for a handsome bank bill. On 14 December she was discussing the possibility of another novel, still toying with the idea of a reworking of *The Professor*, and she can have comforted herself in the winter of 1847–8 with the thought that her future was secure. The tardy publication of *Wuthering Heights* and *Agnes Grey* in an unsatisfactory fashion and Newby's dishonesty in trying to publish them as the works of Currer Bell were slight causes of dissatisfaction, as was the continued decline of Branwell, whose conduct is described on 11 January 1848 as absurd and intolerable.[15]

However there were compensations. Both now and later in less happy times, Charlotte owed a great deal to her publishers. George Smith, the dynamic young head of the firm, does not really enter the Brontë story until the summer of 1848 when Charlotte and Anne visited him to establish their identity. It was his exertions which had rescued the family firm, and we may be fairly sure that it was he who managed the successful publication of *Jane Eyre*. It was he too who recognised the merits of the novel, about which there were, if we are to believe Charlotte's letter to G. H. Lewes on 6 November 1847, some initial reservations.[16] In 1847 Charlotte's dealings were with W. S. Williams, a gentler, more scholarly and less successful man with a large family whom he found it hard to support. Williams was very useful when less good reviews started to come in. Charlotte was angry at the accusations of coarseness which grew for a variety of reasons as 1848 progressed. The association of the wild and wicked *Wuthering Heights* with *Jane Eyre*, carefully fostered by Newby, the fact that periodicals which took longer to deliver their verdict than newspapers were more careful of the need for respectability in view of their family audience, and the rise of nervousness as a result of revolutionary ferment in 1848 produced some harsh verdicts. The main attacks were on the immorality, irreligion and rebelliousness of the Bell novels. Such reviews seem strange to us now, but Rochester is not a moral or religious man, though a little more conventional than Heathcliff, and in preferring him to St John Rivers, Jane was doing more than flout convention.

Jane Eyre went into a second edition in January 1848 and a third in April. The second edition had been dedicated to Thackeray. This was a mistake, as he was married to a mad woman, though not one as unpleasantly mad as Mrs Rochester. In the third edition Charlotte tried to correct the view encouraged by Newby that all the Bells were one person. *Wuthering Heights* was selling and receiving rather baffled reviews, although to Charlotte's chagrin little financial profit for Emily was derived from these sales, whereas she continued throughout 1848 to thank George Smith for regular payments. Although Charlotte and Emily had disagreed over railway shares there is no sign of them quarrelling about the different scale of payment for the novels, and almost certainly Charlotte, who criticised Eliza Reed for meanness in *Jane Eyre*, did something to share her wealth. On 26 February we find her sending some money to Ellen Nussey to whom letters had become less frequent. Charlotte was now busy with other correspondence, and the secret of *Jane Eyre* must have embarrassed her. Letters to Ellen Nussey remain affectionate, but Charlotte seemed to find difficulty in thinking of subjects of conversation. Ellen had been staying with Amelia Ringrose, once engaged to the mad George Nussey, and the conduct of Amelia, eventually to be married to Mary Taylor's brother, provides a boringly normal backcloth to the sensational events of the next five years. Charlotte also discussed matters of Church and State with Ellen in a way that was unusual for her. Her support of the evangelical John Bird Sumner's elevation to the Primacy, and her attacks on the revolutions of 1848 abroad and the agitations of the Chartists at home would have surprised those who thought Currer Bell a seditious atheist.[17]

Charlotte had begun *Shirley* well before 15 February when she says her new book is making slow progress; initially she had tried recasting *The Professor*.[18] Williams would seem to have encouraged her to tackle a public theme. Charlotte's admiration of Thackeray and her dislike – expressed in letters to G. H. Lewes – of Jane Austen might seem to drive her in this direction, although on 28 January she said she must limit her sympathies and cannot penetrate where the very deepest political and social lessons are to be learnt. Events in France and the Chartists in England are of course reflected in *Shirley*, although in a roundabout fashion, as Charlotte focused her novel on the roughly parallel period of the early years of the century when there was constitutional change in France and industrial unrest in Yorkshire.[19]

While Charlotte was slowly beginning *Shirley*, Anne was busy completing *The Tenant of Wildfell Hall*; we do not know what Emily was doing. The theory that she was extending *Wuthering Heights* into a two-volume novel during the second half of 1846 and first half of 1847, even if true, would not explain the absence of any writing in the last year of her life. The theory that the discovery of her poems killed the inspiration in her is fanciful, although it would appear to have been Emily who tried most jealously to protect the anonymity of the Bells, even refusing to admit that Ellis Bell was a woman after Acton and Currer had confessed their sex. It is possible that Emily was engaged upon another novel which has not survived. On 17 February Charlotte wrote to George Smith about the publication of her sisters' future works, regretting that their present engagements to Newby prevented them from accepting any offer by Smith. Two days previously Newby had written to either Emily or Anne urging her not to hurry the completion of the next novel. This letter was found next to an envelope addressed to Ellis Bell, and would fit neatly inside it, although Newby might have confused the two sisters. *The Tenant of Wildfell Hall* was published in June 1848 with advertisements deliberately confusing the three Bells. In view of Newby's dilatoriness in publishing the first novels and his instructions against haste it seems unlikely that the novel of February is *The Tenant of Wildfell Hall*. Newby talked of publishing another work by Ellis and Acton Bell in November 1848.[20]

Perhaps Emily was discouraged from proceeding by the events of July. Newby had tried to sell *The Tenant of Wildfell Hall* to an American publisher as by the author of *Jane Eyre*. George Smith demanded an explanation, and Anne and Charlotte caught the night train to London. The story of their journey is well known, although embellished by such fictional details as the July snowstorm in which they are alleged to have left; they in fact left in a thunderstorm. The details of the journey are supplied in a letter of 4 September 1848. This is the one letter of Charlotte's to Mary Taylor which has survived, although in it she says she has written to Mary many more letters than Mary had returned. The first surviving letter written by Mary to Charlotte is dated 24 July 1848, and says she had received a copy of *Jane Eyre*. There had been correspondence received by Charlotte in June, and clearly Charlotte had discussed her literary ventures with Mary Taylor more freely than with Ellen Nussey. Mary complains eloquently in one of her letters how remote the world of books is from the harsh realities of life in New Zealand. The presence of the Yorkes in *Shirley* is an indication of how Charlotte thought of her absent friend.[21]

The letter to Mary is also an indication of how different our opinion would have been if Charlotte's letters to her had been kept. In spite of some eccentric spelling the letter, in its correct version, has the same nervous energy, brilliant pen portraits and rapidity of action as the novels. Charlotte does not spare either Williams or Smith in her descriptions, although both were, and continued to be, kind to her. The 'tall gentlemanly' Smith did all the talking and made all the arrangements for the Miss Brontës, but it was Williams 'a pale, mild stooping man of fifty', living in a 'comparatively humble but neat residence' who understood immediately the need for the Bells to preserve their anonymity. Charlotte wished Mr Williams to be more practical, and said he lived too much in abstractions, but she did not feel quite at ease with the prosperous George Smith in spite of his scrupulous politeness. Thoughtfully Williams took the two sisters to church, while rather selfishly Smith took them to the opera and dinner to his smart but distant house in Bayswater.[22]

Charlotte felt old and ill at the end of her journey. The delicate Anne must have suffered. In the previous winter all three sisters had been ill with influenza, and grim warnings about Anne's weak chest punctuate the correspondence with Ellen Nussey during 1848. Branwell's correspondence is full of indications of his weakness, and his last poem is a scurrilous lampoon of the Haworth doctor, Doctor Wheelhouse. Nevertheless in spite of a wet summer Charlotte was still fairly cheerful in letters to Ellen Nussey and Miss Wooler in August.[23] In neither letter does she mention her books, although Miss Wooler asked some pointed questions about Cowan Bridge. Anne and Charlotte had seen Newby in London, and, although Anne apparently received little for the copyright of *The Tenant of Wildfell Hall*, Charlotte did not think much of the work. She was annoyed, rightly, when Williams made comparisons between Rochester and Heathcliff, and must have been annoyed by reviews which said that *The Tenant of Wildfell Hall* made it clear that the Bells were a bad lot. It was comforting that Smith Elder agreed to the publication of the poems at the end of the summer.[24]

Events in the autumn drove literary matters out of Charlotte's mind. Branwell's collapse was very sudden. Drink, strongly disapproved of, and drugs, contrary to modern opinion easily available and barely discreditable, had taken their toll of a feeble constitution hardly aided by indifferent medical assistance. Stories about Branwell burning his bed, being dragged back from The Black Bull by Emily and keeping his aged father awake with threats to blow his brains out are of uncertain authority, but life cannot have been easy at Haworth Parsonage. Stories about a deathbed repentance have the authority of Charlotte, although there may be a certain amount of wishful thinking in her letters. Branwell's death on 24 September came with frightful suddenness and Charlotte was badly affected. She was herself very ill and for some time could not answer letters. When she did she was mournful about Branwell's wasted talents. She must too have worried about his immortal soul in spite of the last-minute repentance. The Brontës had been brought up to believe that sinners were punished in Hell, even though the cruelty of the doctrine caused them all to doubt it.[25]

Other worries supervened. In the first letter to Ellen Nussey after Branwell's death (9 October) Charlotte, just recovered from her own illness, said that Emily and Anne were pretty well, but Anne was always delicate and Emily had a cold and cough at present. On 29 October Emily's cold and cough were very obstinate, and Charlotte said she could not shut her eyes to Emily's delicacy of constitution. She had been made apprehensive by Branwell's death. On 7 November, writing to thank George Smith for another remittance and the loan of some books, Charlotte said Emily was too ill to occupy herself with writing. Some harsh reviews painting the Bells as savage monsters were mixed with some very good ones for Charlotte, but neither can have brought such comfort, although she was able to see the irony of the former as she listened to the pathetic painful breathing of her sisters. On 23 November Emily is said to be very ill.[26] An undated letter to Ellen says Charlotte must hope since if she gives way to despair life is worthless. Emily refused to see doctors, although Charlotte tried her best. On 10 December Charlotte told Ellen that hope and fear fluctuated daily, but on 19 December she gave up hope, and on that day Emily died.[27]

Emily's strange death was in keeping with her life. Her refusal of medical aid seems mysterious, but doctors had not done Branwell much good, and Emily may have felt his death even more keenly than Charlotte. The idea that it was the publication of her work that killed Emily does not bear much examination.[28] Charllote's respect for her sister's wish for anonymity, her admiration for her poetry, and her love for her sister are apparent in the years before her death, and naturally grew when Emily was dead. She never quite understood *Wuthering Heights*, although her criticisms of it in letters and in the preface to the second edition are still valuable today.[29] Charlotte had almost finished writing poetry,[30] but her poem on Emily's death shows that the poetry and feeling of her novels could be expressed in verse.

> My darling, thou wilt never know
> The grinding agony of woe
> That we have borne for thee.
> Thus may we consolation tear
> E'en from the depth of our despair
> And wasting misery.
>
> The nightly anguish thou art spared
> When all the crushing truth is bared
> To the awakening mind,
> When the galled heart is pierced with grief
> Till wildly it implores relief,
> But small relief can find.
>
> Nor know'st though what it is to lie
> Looking forth with streaming eye
> On life's lone wilderness.
> 'Weary, weary, dark and drear,
> How shall I the journey bear,
> The burden and distress?'
>
> Then since thou art spared such pain
> We will not wish thee here again;
> He that lives must mourn.
> God help us through our misery
> And give us rest and joy with thee
> When we reach our bourne!

8

Shirley

Christmas never seems to have been celebrated with much rejoicing in the Brontë household, but in 1848, coming so soon after Emily's funeral, it must have been an especially sombre occasion. Anne Brontë did not share Emily's contempt for doctors, but the doctors who visited her could offer little comfort. Mr Brontë was far from well and not unnaturally leant heavily on Charlotte whose letters to Ellen Nussey make painful reading. The symptoms of consumption were the same with Anne as with Emily, and Charlotte, depressed and ill herself, persevered with cod-liver oil, but with little heart. Literature was out of the question. In December there had appeared the famous hostile review by Lady Eastlake in *The Quarterly Review* which said that if the book was written by a woman it was by one who had forfeited the society of her sex. We do not know when Charlotte read this, as she does not mention it until 4 February 1849, but as she gently tended her invalid sister her resentment must have built up.

Ellen Nussey came to stay for a few days in January, and towards the end of the month Anne appeared to rally slightly in the milder weather. On 1 February Charlotte offered to send the first volume of *Shirley* to Williams, apologizing for the fact that cruel reality had snatched her away for so long from the world of imagination, and on 4 February she dispatched the manuscript, asking that it should be read by Smith, Williams and a new figure James Taylor.[1] Both Taylor and Williams made some objections to the beginning of *Shirley*. They disliked the opening with the curates, and complained that the heroes lacked distinctiveness and impressiveness. But in general they were pleased, and indeed the opening of *Shirley* promises much, although it was heavily criticised when it appeared. Charlotte again on 4 February apologized for the lapse in her narrative, and said that it might be hard to resume.

March brought colder weather, and Anne continued to decline. A letter to Miss Wooler on 24 March expresses almost no hope. Anne's wish to go to the seaside, first broached at the end of March, kept Charlotte occupied, and with no noticeable decline in April Charlotte even started to write again. Williams mixed sympathy, practical advice and literary counsel in a judicious fashion, and Charlotte said her principal motive in writing was to please her friends at Cornhill.[2] She did not have much time to write or read, as there was the invalid to nurse, and in other household duties these was but one pair of hands where there used to be three.

On 8 May Charlotte wrote to Williams saying Anne had been first worse and then better. She asked for patience with the writing of *Shirley*, where she had made some little progress, but clearly felt that her publishers expected rather more.[3] For most of May Charlotte was occupied with preparations for the journey to Scarborough with Anne and Ellen Nussey. The whole venture seemed perilous, and indeed turned out to be fatal, but Charlotte's determination to grant her sister's last wish overrode other considerations. And who is to blame her?

The party left Haworth on 24 May and spent the night at York, where Anne was overjoyed to see the Minster. They arrived at Scarborough on the next day, and on 26 May Anne went for a ride on a donkey by the seaside. The next day was a Sunday. Anne was dissuaded from going to Church, but was well enough to go for a short walk in the afternoon. At 11 o'clock on 28 May Anne spoke of feeling a change, discussed her condition calmly with a doctor who said that it was too late to return home, and then at two in the afternoon met her end with Christian fortitude.

The above account is a summary of Ellen Nussey's narrative to Mrs Gaskell.[4] Even after we make allowance for Victorian sentiment Anne's death seems to have been remarkably peaceful and pious. This fact, and the kindness of all concerned, may have consoled Charlotte as she coped with the difficulties of a death and a burial in a strange place. Letters to Williams first from Scarborough and then from Filey spoke of death as a merciful relief.

From Filey Charlotte went with Ellen Nussey to her old friends, the Hudsons, at Easton near Bridlington. She caught cold there, and the contrast between her life in 1849 and the happier visit of 1839, together with the dread of returning home, must have affected her. She reached Haworth on 21 June, and two moving letters to Williams and Ellen Nussey show how difficult she found the empty house.[5]

Charlotte was said, on the authority of Mrs Hudson, to have been writing at Easton. Mrs Gaskell said that chapter 24 of *Shirley*, 'The Valley of the Shadow of Death' was the first to be written after

Anne's death. This may be conjecture, or it may be something that Charlotte told Mrs Gaskell; the spasmodic writing, in which Charlotte had indulged while Anne was still alive, might not have carried her so far, although later she claimed to have written the first two volumes of *Shirley* while Anne was alive.[6] When she returned home she set to work with a will, saying that work was a powerful anodyne to grief, and amazingly she completed *Shirley* by 29 August. She was uncertain of its merits, but did say that the writing of *Shirley* had become a boon to her, taking her out of dark and desolate reality into an unreal and happier region.[7]

Much of Charlotte's life is admirable, but few episodes seem more admirable than her courage and determination in finishing *Shirley*. Twentieth-century students who complain that they cannot complete assessed work because of personal problems would do well to contemplate the example of Charlotte who completed a far greater burden of work facing far more severe problems than most of us are asked to face. Admittedly there was not much else to do. A terribly poignant letter on 14 July to Ellen Nussey talks of 'Solitude', 'Remembrance' and 'Longing' as Charlotte's only companions, and of the clock ticking loudly through the still house. A suggestion by Mr Williams that Charlotte should take a companion was rejected on 26 July by Charlotte who said that she would not like to see youth immured, and that work was her best companion.[8] Mr Brontë fell ill in August, and Charlotte worried about losing the last, the only near and dear relation she had in the world. Otherwise he does not seem to have been all that much comfort to Charlotte. Shared griefs should unite, but all too often the deeply felt emotion cannot find expression, and the unspoken thought divides. Charlotte was not anxious to cause her father anxiety, and kept her author's existence away from him as much as possible. *Jane Eyre* was not mentioned between them more than once a month.[9]

Jane Eyre was, however, a factor in the writing of *Shirley*. In 1848 and in 1849 periodicals continued to review the works of the Brontës. On 16 August Charlotte commented upon a harsh article in *The North British Review* which said that if *Jane Eyre* had been the production of a woman she must be a woman unsexed. The review was contemptuous, as other 1849 reviews were, of the works of Acton and Ellis Bell.[10] The unfairness of these comments bit deeply into Charlotte's soul. Like many authors she would seem to have decided on the title and introduction to her work, not at its commencement, but at its conclusion. *Shirley* only replaced *Field-*

head and *Hollows Mill* in August 1849.[11] The preface seemed a more difficult matter to decide. Charlotte wrote a savage 'Word to *The Quarterly*', full of cruel satire.[12] Her publishers rightly rejected this, urging her instead to make a sad reference to the recent death of Emily and Anne. Charlotte, again one feels rightly, rejected this idea, and *Shirley* eventually appeared without any prefatory note, although hostility to *The Quarterly Review* can still be found in Charlotte's handling of the treatment of governesses in connection with Mrs Pryor.

The manuscript of *Shirley* was collected by Mr Taylor. Charlotte said she could not remember Mr Taylor, and felt that she could not offer any hospitality at Haworth Parsonage. The remoteness of Haworth embarrassed her, but Mr Taylor managed the journey from Scotland to Haworth via Leeds, Keighley and Shipley without the difficulties Charlotte, always a nervous traveller, imagined.

Charlotte anxiously awaited the verdict from Cornhill. Freed from her labours she hoped to see Ellen Nussey, busy with the wedding of her sister Anne at the advanced age of fifty-three to Mr Clapham; this took place on 26 September. Before this date Charlotte had been greatly relieved by a favourable response from her publishers. There were minor objections to the scene when Shirley is bitten by a dog and by the amount of French in the chapter originally entitled 'Le Cheval Dompté', but later changed to 'The First Blue Stocking'. Williams would appear to have been mildly worried by the reception of the book in Yorkshire, and Charlotte made some revisions in her text.[13]

In an interesting reply to a letter expressing this anxiety Charlotte on 21 September declares that she thinks she will escape recognition. She maintains that *Shirley* is far 'less founded on the Real than perhaps appears'. This sentence, together with a similar sentence in a letter to Ellen Nussey of 16 November, 'We only suffer reality to suggest, never to dictate',[14] ought to be written on the fly leaf of every Brontë biography, although *Shirley* is, for a variety of reasons, the most obvious Brontë novel in which we can equate fact and fiction. Indeed in the same letter Charlotte talks of the original of Mr Helstone, Mr Hall and Margaret Hall. In Mr Helstone's case she said that she had only met his original once, but the Halls, modelled on the Healds, the vicar of Birstall and his sister, were a little closer; indeed Miss Heald had on the authority of *The Quarterly Review* violently disapproved of *Jane Eyre*.

The trouble about equating people and places in *Shirley* with people and places in real life is that the circumstances in which the characters find themselves were very different in fiction from what they were in fact. The time is different in the first place. The curates and the Yorke family are thought to be based on Messrs Collins, Bradley and Grant and the Taylor family, but the latter had nothing to do with Luddite riots or the French wars, although the Haworth curates did berate Nonconformists and the Taylors did hold radical views. Mr Helstone is supposed to be based upon Mr Roberson, a stern old Tory whom Charlotte had met in her youth. It is possible that something of Mr Brontë enters into Mr Helstone; the Toryism, disapproval of the French and Nonconformists, the interest in military matters, and even the unfeeling attitude to young women, is something the two men have in common, although Mr Helstone is of course not Caroline's father. Mrs Pryor would seem to be an entirely fictional character and not a very convincing one, either in her behaviour or her conversation or her sudden reappearance. It is alleged that Hortense Moore is basded upon a Mademoiselle Haussé, a teacher in Brussels, but there is no evidence for this.

The four main people in the novel are even harder to link with reality. Robert Moore's resistance against the attempts of the workers to thwart his attempts to introduce machinery to his mills is based upon the exploits of an actual millowner called Cartwright, but his Belgian birth, decisiveness of action and neglect of Caroline point to Monsieur Heger. His brother Louis's profession and gentler nature reveal the other side of Monsieur Heger's nature. Ellen Nussey was rather tartly asked by Charlotte to name the originals of the Moores when she claimed to recognise all the characters apart from the heroines.[15] It is a weakness of the novel that the two heroes, although occasionally contrasted effectively, do seem only to be half characters. Louis's late arrival on the scene and the lack of explanation for Robert's unchivalrous treatment of Caroline are unsatisfactory.

With the two heroines we have some evidence that Caroline was originally modelled on Ellen Nussey, but, as Anne Brontë occupied more and more of Charlotte's attention, so Caroline became more like Anne with even the colour of her eyes changing.[16] Likewise Shirley is supposed to be a more fortunate Emily. It is unlikely that Charlotte would have introduced the Taylors and not mentioned Ellen Nussey, and Caroline's fragility and her neglect by her family is a reminder of Ellen whose home was of course close to the Taylors in the area which is now called Shirley country. Emily and Anne did not live in this part of the world, and, though as Charlotte no doubt thought of her sisters, something of them did enter into the two heroines, we must not be led astray by superficial resemblances like the colour of the eyes or Shirley's dog. Caroline's pathos and her illness, Shirley's courage and her originality are more important resemblances. These must not, however, obscure the vast differences between the heroines of *Shirley* and Charlotte's two sisters, including the fact that Charlotte had to draw entirely upon her own experiences or her imagination when portraying Caroline or Shirley in love, since there is no evidence for Charlotte observing her sisters in this state.

The colour of Caroline Helstone's eyes is, of course, a symptom of the lack of unity which most critics have seen as the besetting fault of *Shirley*, though the general reader is more likely to object to the lack of incident after the dramatic happenings of *Jane Eyre*.[17] Knowledge of the way in which *Shirley* was written provides some excuse for both faults, although Charlotte would have tried to justify the lack of exciting episodes and the lack of coherence in a rather different way. She saw *Shirley* as a representation of truth. Truth, as Oscar Wilde said, is never pure and very rarely simple.[18] Thus a character like Shirley, having bravely stood up for the rights of women, tamely submits to the feeble Louis Moore. The silly curates and the stern Helstone, so wrong in many things, turn out to be in the right when it comes to dealing with the workers and the Nonconformists, joining with Caroline and Shirley to rout them. Robert Moore is right to suppress the violence of the Luddites, but is unfeeling and shortsighted when it comes to improving their conditions. Mrs Pryor is a downtrodden governess, but speaks without sarcasm of the right of the aristocracy to lay down the law.

Brave efforts have been made to solve not the only inconsistency of individual characters, but the incoherence of the different sets of characters. Women, governesses and the poor are seen as the underdogs in this particular novel, and the difficulties of righting their lot are honestly shown. People such as Shirley do their best and win a few victories against the curates and the snobbish Sympsons, but in general the establishment is too powerful and compromise is necessary – as is shown by the unromantic conclusion after the not very exciting marriages. Charlotte's statement about the position of women is perhaps the strongest of her attacks on the establishment, and certainly the most topical. It is interesting to note how the novel begins with the curates ordering about their landladies as if they were objects, not people; it is the same curates who imagine themselves as lady-killers, but are no match even for Shirley's dog. Caroline Helstone's indignant reply to her uncle's refusal to take seriously her claims for work is to ask whether she should play with her doll. Charlotte's treatment of the old spinsters, Miss Ainley and Miss Mann, is neither sentimental nor sympathetic, but realistic and original. These insights more than make up for the tame conclusion to the novel.

Interestingly in letters about early reviews of the novel Charlotte was disappointed that the question of Currer Bell's sex was raised. In a letter of 6 November to James Taylor she says 'Speaking for myself alone I do wish that the hirelings of the press were still ignorant of my being a woman.'[19] To G. H. Lewes on 1 November she had declared 'I wish you did not think me a woman. I wish all reviewers believed "Currer Bell" to be a man.'[20] Lewes's review of *Shirley*, in January 1850, perversely took Charlotte at her word, but hardly to her advantage when he said, 'A more masculine book in the sense of vigour was never written. Indeed that vigour often amounts to coarseness – and it is certainly the very antipode to ladylike.'[21]

Reviews of the Brontës had continued to be written during the year and a half between the publication of *The Tenant of Wildfell Hall* and *Shirley*, and many had seized upon the charge of coarseness as an accusation that could be made against the Bells. They tried the same thing with *Shirley* in spite of the lack of many scenes which could possibly be called coarse. There is little in *Shirley* that is sexually provocative, and reviews had to fall back on Shirley whistling or quotations from scripture out of context. Possibly some reviews did feel that Charlotte had some uncomfortable things to say about the position of women, and, unable or unwilling to examine their own prejudices, used coarseness as a blanket term to express their discomfort.

On the whole, given that most modern readers feel that *Shirley* is something of a failure after *Jane Eyre*, and that most contemporary readers were unaware of the circumstances in which *Shirley* was written, it is surprising that it got off so lightly. It is possible that Smith Elder did try to shield their author by sending her only the kinder reviews, and in general the periodicals treated *Shirley* less kindly than the newspapers, whose favourable reception pleased Charlotte so much in November.[22]

It is also possible that someone at Smith Elder discreetly let reviewers know something of Charlotte's sad story. We find both Thackeray and Mrs Gaskell in October 1849 speculating about the identity of Currer Bell, and in December – when Charlotte went to London – they found out the answer. In London the Smiths introduced Charlotte to literary circles, including many critics.[23] When Charlotte returned to Yorkshire she soon discovered that she was well known there. This angered her. She told Ellen on 19 January 1850 that the notoriety of *Shirley* in Dewsbury was as good as an emetic to her, and on 16 February said that the Haworth people had been making great fools of themselves about *Shirley*. The enthusiasm of Mr Nicholls and Martha Brown for the book aroused her pity and her contempt.[24]

It was, of course, Charlotte's Yorkshire audience who were most keen to equate fact with fiction, and indeed it is in Yorkshire today that this tradition persists in spite of the careful efforts by the Brontë Society to distinguish the two. Charlotte's two disclaimers to Williams and Ellen Nussey occurred before she was aware of the Yorkshire reaction, and it was not to avoid embarrassment that she told Ellen Nussey that the characters in *Shirley* were not literal portraits.

A little inconsistently Charlotte was angry with newspaper critics who did not know her circumstances and angry with Yorkshire critics too eager to use their knowledge of Charlotte's circumstances to criticise the novel. Her sensitivity to criticism after some of the hostile criticism of 1848 is perfectly understandable. Charlotte probably knew that *Shirley* was inferior to *Jane Eyre*, and this knowledge as well as her personal circumstances must have coloured her reaction. Most of us are more defensive when we have more to defend.

Shirley was not, however, a failure. Some readers, such as Mrs Gaskell's friend Catherine Winkworth, preferred it to *Jane Eyre*.[25] A novel with obvious links to a particular time and place, it has lasted less well than the universal *Jane Eyre*, but it is wrong to dismiss it as a mere *roman-à-clef* about Charlotte's Yorkshire acquaintances. Its most interesting theme is the treatment of women, and here Charlotte was very definitely not writing about her own experience since with the success of *Shirley* she was now assured of a regular income and employment as a novelist. Mary Taylor also found *Shirley* more interesting than *Jane Eyre*.[26] This is not surprising in view of the connection between the Yorkes and the Taylors, but in addition Mary held what were for the time very advanced feminist views. In April 1850 she wrote to Charlotte sternly as follows.

I have seen some extracts from Shirley in which you talk of women writing. And this first duty, this great necessity you seem to think that *some* women may indulge in – if they give up marriage and don't make themselves too disagreeable to the opposite sex. You are a coward and a traitor. A woman who works is by that alone better than one who does not and a woman who does not happen to be rich and who still earns no money and does not wish to do so, is guilty of a great fault – almost a crime – A dereliction of duty which leads rapidly and almost certainly to all manner of degradation. It is very wrong of you to plead for toleration for workers on the ground of their being in peculiar circumstances and few in number and singular in disposition. Work or degradation is the lot of all except the very small number born to wealth.[27]

We do not know what Charlotte made of this advice. In New Zealand at the same time were people who thought that Miss Brontë was savage with the curates because she had been jilted by one of them.[28] The expectation that marriage was the natural lot of all women was the prevailing mood of Victorian times, and Mary Taylor's view that women should work was exceptional. In the next three years of her life Charlotte tried to work, but the pull of marriage still caused her difficulties.

9

Villette

On 29 November 1849 Charlotte visited London, staying with the Smiths at Westbourne Place, returning on 15 December. While in London she visited the Wheelwrights in Lower Phillimore Place, Kensington, but spent most of her time with the Smiths. This visit was important, as we have seen, in establishing Charlotte's literary identity. It is also possible to see it as important in sowing the first seeds of *Villette*, although here again we must be very careful in distinguishing fact and fiction.

Monsieur Heger has tended to rule the roost in discussions of *Villette*, and, as we have shown, the equation between him and Paul Emanuel is not an exact one. Three people whom Charlotte saw at close quarters during her visit in 1849 are also linked with *Villette*. We have already discussed the similarities, and dissimilarities between Laetita Wheelwright and Paulina de Basompierre. Charlotte did say that Paulina was entirely imaginary.[1] Laetitia was now twenty-one, having been fourteen when Charlotte first met her. These ages are not the same as those of Paulina, never precisely specified, but surely younger than Laetitia's, but the renewal of acquaintance is a similarity that should not be overlooked. In *Villette* Charlotte makes John Bretton fall in love with Paulina. She could have dwelt on the possibility of a similar event happening as she visited the Smiths and the Wheelwrights. Dr Wheelwright knew about the firm of Smith Elder, but this is about the only evidence we have of any connection between the two. George Smith was indignant when Charlotte suggested that she might stay with the Wheelwrights rather than with him.

George Smith and his mother had, as has been shown, something in common with John Graham and Mrs Bretton, although as a famous author Charlotte was very different from the unkown Lucy Snowe. Another character – whose part in *Villette* has been insufficiently recognised – is James Taylor; he had arrived at Haworth to collect the manuscript of *Shirley*, an important and yet unappreciated task not totally dissimilar from the role of Paul Emanuel in deciding Lucy's future on her arrival at the Rue Isabelle.

Soon after his arrival Charlotte wrote to Ellen about 'the little man', saying that he was rigid, despotic and self-willed, and that he tried to be kind but failed.

> He has a determined, dreadful nose in the middle of his face which when pushed into my countenance cuts into my soul like iron. Still he is horribly intelligent, quick, startling, sagacious and with a memory of relentless tenacity. To turn to Williams after him, or to Smith himself, is to turn from granite to easy down or warm fur.[2]

Sometimes, even when writing to Ellen Nussey, Charlotte writes as a poetic novelist rather than as a prosaic recounter of events. Her description to her father of her meeting with Thackeray is much more tedious. Ellen would appear to have been excited by Charlotte's letter, but Charlotte urged her to dismiss the twenty romantic notions she had formed. The dismissal, like the protruding nose, may indicate an embarrassment if not a love-affair. In the same letter to Ellen Nussey, Charlotte reports that Mr Taylor has fallen victim to rheumatic fever and that she is sorry for his sake.[3]

In London Charlotte met Thackeray; neither party gained a great deal from the meeting. She also met Harriet Martineau, and the initial acquaintance looked promising. Charlotte's stern puritan upbringing found it hard to accommodate itself to the London literary establishment, but found no difficulty in connecting itself with contemporary radical thinkers. Harriet Martineau, who happened to be staying very close to the Smiths in Westbourne Street, was an odd and not totally suitable friend for Charlotte. Born in 1802 of a Unitarian shopkeeping background she had earned a certain amount of both fame and fortune through her tales of life in the difficult years of the Industrial Revolution. She then visited America, wrote a full-length novel, *Deerbrook* – thought far superior to *Shirley* by Catherine Winkworth – and suffered a nervous breakdown, from which she did not recover until June 1844. Initially, as two famous women writers who both had a strong religious background, who had suffered personal distress, and who loved the Lake District, Harriet Martineau and Charlotte Brontë got on famously. Time was to show up the differences.

Charlotte reached home on 15 December 1849. In the space of a year she had lost both her sisters, published a second novel and visited London in circumstances quite undreamt of when she and her sisters first put pen to paper. Letters to Ellen Nussey and Williams on 19 December show up the stark contrast between energetic days in London and weary ones in Haworth. Charlotte knew she had to live at Haworth for most of the year, and in tracing the course of *Villette* we should not forget the shaping consciousness of Charlotte, like Lucy Snowe, curiously involved with and at the same time detached from the characters she encountered.

Ellen Nussey came to stay at the end of December. Her faithful friendship is the subject of a letter to W. S. Williams on 3 January 1850 in which Charlotte comments on Ellen's good nature but lack of literary sensibility.[4] Lewes and Thackeray wrote letters, unfortunately not preserved, and Sir James Kay Shuttleworth called. Sir James was a man of remarkable energy, living only about ten miles from Haworth. After threatening a visit at the end of January he called at the beginning of March and persuaded Charlotte to visit his house at Gawthorpe in the middle of the month. As a doctor, social reformer and educationist Sir James was naturally interested in Charlotte, although his interest became at times tiresome. Charlotte frequently comments on his ill health, and he would have made a good subject for a work of fiction, but Charlotte did not write about him. It is difficult to find any evidence of Charlotte being involved in any literary activity at this time. She was still reading reviews of *Shirley*, and there were plans to bring out a cheap edition of *Jane Eyre*. Williams faithfully supplied parcels of books, including some novels by Jane Austen.

Charlotte went to Ellen Nussey, who had been ill, on 18 April, and on her return on 22 April found her father far from well. This illness lasted until the middle of May and caused the postponement of a visit to London in the company of the Kay Shuttleworths. Then Sir James himself fell ill with some most alarming symptoms, but on 30 May Charlotte again visited London to stay with the Smiths who had moved to 76 Gloucester Terrace. The visit lasted until 25 June and was followed by a visit to Scotland with the Smiths. Again Charlotte told Ellen not to read too much into this prolonged acquaintance, and refused to accompany George Smith to the West Coast of Scotland, merely spending two days in early July in Edinburgh. Charlotte had spent the intervening period between London and Scotland with Ellen Nussey, and it was to Brookroyd that she returned from Edinburgh.

Charlotte stayed at Brookroyd for a few more days, and returned to Haworth in the middle of July. Her father had been alarmed by rumours of her impending marriage and reports of ill health. Charlotte was able to discount the first cause of alarm. She found life at home difficult after the excitements of the previous six weeks, and complained later of awful solitude and the craving for companionship. Memories of Scotland and London remained strong. Redecoration at the Parsonage meant that Charlotte had much to do at home. The arrival of Richmond's portrait, a flatteringly romantic one, and a picture of the Duke of Wellington as a present from George Smith aroused a flurry of correspondence, Charlotte writing three letters to him in four days.[5]

Clearly Charlotte was restless, and on 18 August she was off on her travels again, this time to Windermere in the company of the Kay Shuttleworths. The Lake District had obvious attractions for Charlotte and the scenery more than compensated for the difficult journey and her dislike of her philistine host in spite of his politeness. This visit was an important one as Charlotte met Mrs Gaskell. In the absence of her hostess the two authoresses saw a great deal of each other. Mrs Gaskell found out many parts of Charlotte's story and wrote vivid descriptions of this to her friends. First impressions are important, and the view Mrs Gaskell formed of Charlotte on this first meeting coloured her final account; she emphasises perhaps too much in her first letters the peculiarities of Mr Brontë, deriving much of her information from Lady Kay Shuttleworth, the loneliness of Charlotte's journeys to Belgium with no mention of the fact that Emily accompanied her, and the desolation of Charlotte's present existence.[6]

On her return Charlotte, a year after completing *Shirley*, at last found the opportunity of some literary work. The appearance in *The Palladium* of a highly appreciative article by Sidney Dobell on *Wuthering Heights*, maintaining that this novel was by the author of *Jane Eyre*, may have been the pretext for a suggestion by Williams that Charlotte should reiissue *Wuthering Heights* and *Agnes Grey* with a short biographical introduction. It was Taylor who drew Charlotte's attention to the article in *The Palladium*; George Smith was at hand to deal with Newby. By 20 September Charlotte had written a rough draft of the notice about her sisters. On 29 September she said that she was going to write a special preface to *Wuthering Heights* and to modify some of the Yorkshire peculiarities of the dialogue. On 13 September she had suggested adding a few poems by both Anne and Emily, but we hear curiously little of this part of her task.[7]

As an editor of and commentator on her sisters' work Charlotte has won little praise. Her refusal to republish *The Tenant of Wildfell Hall* as something 'hardly desirable to preserve' may be a reaction against the savage reviews of 1848, but Charlotte's lack of appreciation of Anne, conspicuous in the biographical notice, existed before this time. The preface to *Wuthering Heights* is more discerning, with Charlotte striking an interesting balance between the baffled response of contemporary readers and the ecstatic appreciation of modern critics. To the poems we have seen that Charlotte did not pay a great deal of attention. She chose only a few, edited them to suit her own and Victorian taste, and did not select some of the more interesting ones. The desire to protect her sisters' memory and the need to eliminate Gondal or personal references should be borne in mind. It should also be remembered that going through the works of her sisters within two years of their deaths was for Charlotte a painful experience. She said as much to both Ellen Nussey and Williams in letters of September and October, which make distressing reading, saying how the work had brought on pangs of bereavement.[8]

In the letter to Ellen Nussey, Charlotte declared that she 'had thought to find occupation and interest in writing at home' but that in 'the deficiency of every stimulus her efforts had been in vain'. In more cheerful spirits she wrote to Smith, Taylor and Williams long letters between 31 October and 9 November, chiefly concerned with religious matters.[9] The election of Cardinal Wiseman to the Archbishopric of Westminster in 1850 aroused Charlotte's anti-Catholic prejudices, which are also conspicuous in *Villette*. Charlotte's Broad Church sympathies are revealed by her praise of Dr Arnold, whose widow Charlotte had met in the Lake District, and was to meet again in December.

On 16 December 1850 Charlotte visited another inhabitant of the Lake District, Harriet Martineau. She spent a week there with apparent enjoyment in spite of the austere habits of her hostess who rose at five each morning and took a cold bath. Charlotte wrote to Ellen Nussey from Ambleside on 18 December saying she had recovered from the depression of the autumn.[10] It is possible, since little other entertainment was offered at Miss Martineau's house, that Charlotte made some progress with writing during this week, although this was more likely to be work on *The Professor* rather than on *Villette*. Sir James Kay Shuttleworth tried to press Charlotte to stay, but she returned to spend Christmas with Ellen before coming back to Haworth on 27 December.

She wrote a great deal about Harriet Martineau and something about the Arnolds. Harriet Martineau had made a good impression, although there were subjects on which she and Charlotte differed, probably religious subjects. Matthew Arnold, though he improved upon acquaintance, made a less favourable impact; his foppery and unsettled theological opinions disturbed Charlotte. Charlotte wrote more long letters to James Taylor and George Smith. She told Ellen that there was no chance of her marrying Smith, some seven years her junior, and indeed there seems to have been no such chance. With the little man, as Charlotte rather facetiously called Taylor, there seemed more hope. On 30 January she said there was a quiet constancy about him which added a foot to his stature, although distance and respect were preserved.[11]

Meanwhile Smith Elder had given their verdict on *The Professor*. It is not clear how much extra work Charlotte had done on recasting her first novel, or exactly what Smith and Williams said when they received the revised version, or how disappointed Charlotte was when her publishers did not seem very enthusiastic. Charlotte wrote to Williams on 1 February expressing relief, possibly because she thought quite highly of *The Professor*, and to Smith on 5 February saying that the novel had been rejected nine times by publishers, although this last occasion had been a nominal acceptance.[12] Charlotte had offered *The Professor* twice before to Smith Elder, once after the publication of *Jane Eyre*. The manuscript shows signs of two different revisions.[13]

It is unfortunately impossible to say how much work Charlotte did on *The Professor* in the winter of 1850–1. Clearly work on *The Professor* is important for the study of the genesis of *Villette*, since looking at her previous novel must have reminded Charlotte of Belgium and locking the Professor in a cupboard by himself, to use Charlotte's own quaint phrase, must have cleared the way for her major novel. By February 1851 Charlotte had not written anything important for a year and a half, and it is possible to trace the beginnings of impatience in her publishers. Charlotte talks of her own dilatoriness to Williams in the letter of 1 February, and says to Smith that she should be in solitary confinement until she had written a book.

The letters to Smith are full of banter, a marked contrast to the formal politeness of letters to Taylor. Charlotte, for example, talks to Smith of her fondness for invitations from baronets when it is clear that there was nothing she liked less than the pressing claims of Sir James Kay Shuttleworth. To Taylor she gravely denounced Harriet Martineau's latest book as 'the first exposition of avowed atheism and materialism' she had ever read.[14] An interesting letter to Smith of 11 March comments on a suggestion he seems to have made that she should take Cornhill as the subject of her writing. Charlotte reassured Smith that they were all safe from Currer Bell – 'safe from his satire – safer still from his eulogism'. Charlotte continues with some further words which again ought to be etched into the brain of anyone too eager to read her works as autobiography.

> We cannot (or at least I cannot) write of our acquaintance with the consciousness that others will recognize their portraits, or that they themselves will know the hand which has sketched them.[15]

And yet while writing this Charlotte was engaged, like her heroine Lucy Snowe, in two half romances, in which the imagination of a lonely woman made much of unspoken thoughts. In the same letter to George Smith, Charlotte comments calmly on the proposal to set up a branch of Smith Elder in India with Taylor as its manager. Taylor came to Haworth for a short visit at the end of March or beginning of April. Charlotte, in a letter to Ellen Nussey of 5 April, read much into his keen looks at her, and thought little of his appearance. Mr Brontë got on very well with Charlotte's suitor, if suitor he was. Four days later she said she felt more gently to him now that he had left. On 12 April Charlotte's main preoccupation seemed her father's health, but there is a baffling reference to a 'crumbling away of a seeming formation of support and prospect of hope'.[16]

Taylor did not leave England until 20 May 1851. On 23 April he wrote to Charlotte suggesting a meeting in London before that time. Charlotte said there was still 'a want of plain mutual understanding in this business, and . . . sadness and pain in more ways than one'.[17] It is difficult to know what had happened. Had Charlotte expected a formal proposal by 12 April and not received one? Did she reproach herself for not giving Taylor more encouragement? On 23 April she said that Mr Taylor was not gentlemanly enough for her to accept him as a husband. This suggests a proposal and a refusal, but both may have been hypothetical. On 5 May Charlotte said that Mr Brontë had favoured Mr Taylor. Surprisingly, in view of Mr Brontë's snobbery and later hostility to Mr Nicholls, Mr Brontë had no patience with Charlotte's objections that Taylor was no gentleman. Charlotte and Mr Brontë did not talk openly, but she guessed, perhaps rightly, that, since Taylor was in India, an engagement with him would be a long-standing affair, and would therefore cause no immediate trouble for Mr Brontë.[18]

Charlotte was clearly disturbed by the experience, and something of Mr Taylor's small stature, harsh manners and long absence worked their way into *Villette*, about the writing of which we hear nothing in these months. Meanwhile George Smith was attentive, offering Charlotte the chance to travel – like a Thackeray heroine – on the Rhine. This she refused, as she also refused an invitation from another young admirer, Sidney Dobell, to go to Switzerland. Sidney Dobell was twenty-seven and safely married. George Smith was more of an attraction, and it was presumably anxiety about her father's health that kept Charlotte from going abroad, as she did go to London to stay with the Smiths from 28 May to 27 June.

In London she led a life very different from the lonely existence of Haworth. Visits to lectures by Thackeray, the Crystal Place and Somerset House all took place before 2 June. On 7 June Charlotte went to see the famous French actress Rachel, an episode relived in describing Vashti in *Villette*. On 11 June Charlotte complained of a sick headache, and was clearly not well for much of her visit. A constant stream of visitors depressed and tired Charlotte. It is worth repeating again before trying to link too many of the events in London with the writing of *Villette* that, unlike Lucy Snowe, Charlotte was not an unknown schoolteacher, but a famous writer, much in demand by aristocratic and literary society. She left London later than she had wished, returning via Mrs Gaskell's house in Manchester to Haworth on 30 June.

On 1 July she wrote an important letter to Smith, which appears to refer to some kind of agreement to write a new novel. She wrote two more letters in the next week, in the last saying she had quite expected the correspondence to be broken off.[19] This may seem to foreshadow John Graham, but it is difficult to pierce the veil of facetiousness, very different from the tone of Lucy Snowe, with which Charlotte addressed her publisher. The slightly strained note which appears in the correspondence may not betoken any trace of a love-affair, since both Smith and Charlotte were in an awkward position owing to the lapse in time between the completion of *Shirley* and Charlotte's next novel.

In August Charlotte appeared to be trying to interest Smith in publishing works by Mrs Gaskell and Harriet Martineau. On 1 September she reported some ill health in Ellen Nussey. Two mentions of a serial in September suggest that Smith was trying to coax Charlotte to write in this form, but she refused. The visit of a Branwell cousin in September and Miss Wooler in October, and the ill health of the servants Tabby and Martha in that month, were further distractions. In a letter of October she talks over painful mental worry, and on 6 November, writing to Mrs Gaskell, she mentions annual depression around the equinox.

Charlotte refused invitations in October to Harriet Martineau, Mrs Gaskell and Mrs Forster, Thomas Arnold's eldest daughter. All lived comparatively close, and, though she made excuses about the health of the servants and her father, and about her anxiety to avoid causing offence by declining one invitation and refusing another, her real reason for enduring solitude at home was the wish to get on with her writing.

Taylor wrote on 17 September and 2 October. Charlotte wrote politely, if not enthusiastically, a letter in reply on 15 November, going over the events of the summer in a dutiful fashion, but concluding by saying that she had ceased to expect a letter.[20]

On 20 November we at last hear of some progress on *Villette*. Charlotte told Smith that she had been able to work a little lately, but did not intend to compete with the coming works of Thackeray and Harriet Martineau. This meant that Smith should not expect anything until the autumn of 1852 and that Charlotte must remain at home to write. Smith must have persuaded her to name an earlier date, for on 28 November Charlotte said that it was not at all likely her book would be ready by the date she had mentioned. She complained of ill health and of long periods when inspiration was lacking. She also told Smith not to advertise her novel in advance.[21]

The winter of 1851–2 was perhaps the worst that Charlotte had suffered since Emily's death. The weather was severe and Charlotte's health was bad. Apart from one visit to Brookroyd in January she remained solidly at Haworth for almost a year, trying to write. In November she told Smith that she was not very pleased with what she had written so far. Harriet Martineau's book *Oliver Weld*, recommended by Charlotte to Smith Elder, was not welcomed very warmly, and Charlotte felt an added reason for guilt.[22] Bravely she kept in touch with Ellen Nussey and Miss Wooler exchanging news about Mary Taylor in New Zealand and Amelia Taylor in Hunsworth. Her symptoms about which she told Ellen, who visited her in

January, sounded alarming, her medicines more so; doses of mercury made her mouth and tongue ulcerated, and at times she was hardly capable of speaking or swallowing anything more than half a teacupful of liquid a day.[23] She went to Brookroyd with a low intermittent fever, but apparently recovered. As well as her illness, solitude and depression continued to rack her. A letter to Mrs Gaskell on 6 February talks of lack of sleep, loss of appetite and ghastly dreams.[24] It seems impossible that Charlotte could have thought of literature at such a time, and yet *Villette* is a novel full of sleeplessness and nightmares.

Smith, whose attentiveness to his author deserves high praise, sent her the manuscript of *Henry Esmond*, on which Charlotte made some sound criticisms. Writing on 12 March Charlotte refused an invitation from Miss Wooler on the grounds that her work had lain untouched since she had been ill, and on 21 March she told Smith to expect no good of Currer Bell that summer.[25] Ellen Nussey suggested a visit but Charlotte refused. She also refused to go to Sussex with Ellen in May, instead travelling by herself to Filey in June.

In May Charlotte would appear to have said that she had heard nothing from Taylor, and expected to hear nothing. This seems the best interpretation of some rather veiled references in a letter to Ellen Nussey dated 4 May 1852.[26] There is another rather odd statement in a letter of 6 June to the effect that there were reasons why she should visit Filey instead of going to the South, by which she presumably meant Sussex rather than London.[27] The visit to Filey was concerned with literature, rather than love. To Miss Wooler she said that her work had stood obstinately still for some time, and even at Filey Charlotte suffered slightly from depression, but after a month had recovered her spirits.

Her troubles were, however, not over. Mr Brontë fell ill shortly after Charlotte's return, and on 28 July she had again to appeal to Williams not to announce any impending work. Ellen Nussey was all the summer in Sussex, and though letters continued to pass between the friends some sort of constraint seemed to enter into them. Charlotte eventually broke through and said she was silent because she had nothing to say, that her life was a pale blank and often a weary burden and that the future sometimes appalled her.[28]

She wrote this and other sad remarks about her loneliness in a letter of 25 August at home when she must have been working on her lonely heroine. In September Ellen returned from Sussex, and Charlotte, in spite of her claims that her work was still going slowly, invited her to stay for a week in October: the visit seemed to cheer Charlotte up. At the end of the month she sent the first two volumes of *Villette* to Smith, full of doubt as to how it would be received. Much to her relief Smith replied with admirable promptness, giving a generally favourable verdict, and of course insisting against Charlotte's modest objections that the novel must be published as being written by Currer Bell.

Smith had some reservations about some discrepancies in John Graham's character, the want of harmony between his boyhood and manhood, and the abrupt change of his feelings towards Ginevra Fanshawe. At this stage Smith probably thought Graham was to be the hero of the work, and Charlotte explained on 3 November that most of the third volume was to be given up to the 'crabbed professor' as she called Paul Emanuel.[29] This change of focus was rather to shock Smith as it shocks most first-time readers who have not had the benefit of this warning. Williams was also polite; he had more difficulties with the heroine whose name changed from Snowe to Frost to Snowe again. Williams said she might be thought both morbid and weak, unless more of her history was revealed.

To this Charlotte replied bravely that Lucy Snowe was both morbid and weak at times.[30] It is one of the great strengths of the book that we penetrate Lucy Snowe's coldness to see her inner fire; Charlotte said that her cold name was given on the *lucus a non lucendo* principle. It is also a great and original achievement to paint a heroine who appears admirable in spite of her weakness, and, as Charlotte did in the third volume, to turn the petty and boring martinet which Paul Emanuel appears on first sight into the admirable and human being with whom the novel concludes. Something of the strength of Charlotte's writing in *Villette* appears in the two letters which Charlotte sent in reply to the criticisms of her publishers, and it is not altogether surprising that she finished the novel so rapidly, dispatching it on 20 November. When she had completed the book which had cost her so much pain she said her prayers.[31]

She then visited Ellen Nussey at Brookroyd. Smith did not reply immediately, and Charlotte thought of going up to London. She was a little stern in a letter to Smith of 6 December for the slight delay, and in a slightly mercenary fashion complained to Miss Wooler on 7 December that Smith had not raised the fee for her novel from the five hundred pounds she had received for *Shirley*. To Smith, Charlotte agreed that the character of Paulina was not very substantial, and interestingly said 'the fault lies in its wanting the germ of the real – in its being purely imaginary'.[32]

When Charlotte says the character of Paulina has nothing of the real in it, she suggests that other characters do have something, and in this chapter we have tried to show how reality impinged upon fiction, although concentrating more on the years 1851 and 1852 than the years 1842 and 1843. Clearly Belgium and Monsieur Heger do enter into *Villette*, and Charlotte's loneliness in these years may have reminded her of her isolation in Belgium. Various models have been suggested for Ginevra Fanshawe.[33] Taylor and Smith, the hectic life of London and the ticking of the clock at Haworth, also play their part. Charlotte was lonely and depressed like Lucy Snowe. Like Lucy Snowe she was able to emerge from the shadows and create something. Her creation was not a successful school but a great novel, hacked out of illness and despair. We should salute her achievement while noting wryly the rather prosaic way in which Charlotte reacted to it by complaining of delay and lack of money. Waiting round the corner after Charlotte's poetic novel was a prosaic romance.

10

Wife

With the publication of *Villette* Charlotte's life as a creative writer was virtually at an end. Her one remaining major fragment, *Emma*, tells of how a poor little rich girl arrives at a school, and it is then found that she is a poor little poor girl since her fees are not paid.[1] This opening scene is full of interest, but it is impossible to guess how the story is going to develop. Orphan children and schools feature prominently in the other novels, and the story is reminiscent of some of the juvenilia, notably *Ashworth*, but this fact hardly helps us to conjecture the possible outcome of *Emma*. It would be interesting to know whether it was the child or the teachers who were going to provide the main focus of the story, but we would not get very far in speculating about the possible outline of *Villette* if we had only its first chapter, and the future development of *Emma* must remain a mystery. Another fragment entitled *Willie Ellin*, also written in 1853, probably belongs to the same story.[2]

Most of the interest in Charlotte's last two and a half years must, therefore, be biographical and not literary. The strange story of Mr Nicholls's courtship, which had already begun before *Villette* was published, has no direct connection with any major work that Charlotte wrote. Indeed, though it was a strange, sad story – and Charlotte wrote some strange, sad stories – this is about the only resemblance between art and life. Perhaps this is one reason why the story needs telling. Another excuse for spending time on Mr Nicholls is that, though he is a comparatively uninteresting character who had little impact upon Charlotte's writing or reputation, his courtship and marriage did involve Mr Brontë, Ellen Nussey and Mrs Gaskell, all of whom are extremely important in Charlotte's life.

One of the difficulties about describing the story of Charlotte's marriage is that clearly we do not have all the evidence before us. Ellen Nussey must have destroyed some letters, since between 20 June 1853 and 1 March 1854, after a brisk series of letters in which Mr Nicholls's chances seemed fairly poor, there is only one letter, uncertainly dated, and not very interesting since it mainly deals with household effects. On 11 April 1854 Charlotte announced her engagement, after writing another series of letters in which Mr Nicholls's chances appear progressively better.[3]

Mrs Gaskell, the first recipient of Ellen Nussey's letters, did herself visit Haworth in September 1853, and left a moving account of her visit, although with only a discreet mention of Mr Nicholls as a great anxiety on Charlotte's mind. After their marriage Mr Nicholls asked Charlotte to tell Ellen to destroy her letters. Ellen apparently said she would, but on somewhat specious grounds did not keep her promise. The quarrel between Charlotte's husband and her oldest friend is extremely important for students of her life, and is an additional motive for writing this chapter. For the moment it is worth noting that Ellen, probably out of guilt that she had not fulfilled her pledge to Mr Nicholls, or possibly as a result of some previous pledge to Charlotte herself, did destroy much of the evidence in the vital period of the courtship, although she preserved most of Charlotte's correspondence.

Fortunately Charlotte did write to other correspondents, and equally fortunately there is enough evidence in the letters to Ellen Nussey before and after the lacuna in the correspondence to her for us to be able to piece together what happened. Neither Mr Brontë nor Mr Nicholls nor Ellen Nussey emerges with any particular credit from the following pages; Charlotte, on the other hand, appears to have behaved throughout with dignity and consideration in the difficult position she found herself.

When on 13 December 1852 Mr Nicholls stumbled through his embarrassing proposal, faithfully recounted in a letter to Ellen Nussey two days later, Charlotte was thirty-six, almost, but not quite, in staid Victorian times, at the age when marriage was improbable. She had in six difficult years produced three books, each of which had earned her more than twice her father's annual income. Mrs Gaskell commented on the way the Parsonage had been improved as a result of Charlotte's wealth. Her future fame and prosperity were assured; her future happiness was not. The loss of her sisters, the loneliness of the past two years, her father's age and ill health, the knowledge of her age, her craving to give and receive love must have made her desperately vulnerable. And yet initially Mr Nicholls provided no temptation.

Mr Nicholls was two years younger than Charlotte. He had arrived at Haworth in 1845, a year of crisis in the Brontë household dominated by Branwell's disgrace, the threat of Mr Brontë's blindness and Charlotte's final realisation that Monsieur Heger was not for her. In the intervening seven years the triumphs and tragedies of the Brontë household kept Charlotte from taking much notice of Mr Nicholls. He is supposed to have appeared in the guise of Mr Macarthey in *Shirley* – not a silly character like the other curates, but not exactly praised either. In July 1846 Charlotte coldly denies any rumour that she is going to be married to Mr Nicholls, saying that 'a cold far-away sort of civility are the only terms on which I have ever been with Mr Nicholls'.[4] Possibly Mr Nicholls did not feel the same, and his chances of aspiring to Charlotte's hands must have seemed greater in 1846 when she was unknown and faced with an uncertain future as a governess, than when she was a famous authoress in 1852. He may have felt Charlotte's loneliness, and he may have felt that long years of helping the Brontës through their troubles had earned him some reward.

If so he was to be rudely disappointed. Charlotte had written of Mr Nicholls on his first arrival in Haworth that he was a respectable young man and appears not to have altered that opinion. She claimed to Ellen Nussey that she had had vague misgivings about the behaviour of Mr Nicholls. With hindsight she must have recognised the symptoms of his passion, but not until he knocked on her door instead of leaving after an hour-long discussion with her father did she realise what was before her. He stammered through his declaration; she said she would let him have an answer on the next day. Mr Nicholls left, and Charlotte went to see Mr Brontë who was inordinately angry, and persuaded Charlotte to promise that she would give Mr Nicholls a distinct refusal on the next day.

Mr Brontë's anger, which persisted until the day of the wedding, some eighteen months later, may seem hard to explain. Charlotte could not understand it, and the degree of opposition she encountered may have persuaded her to look more favourably on Mr Nicholls. Her heroines, unlike herself, had been poor and obscure, and won their way through difficulty and hostility to marry her heroes who, unlike Mr Nicholls, were powerful and masterful men. The obstacles which Mr Nicholls encountered in his courtship may have enabled Charlotte to see him in a more romantic light.

Mr Brontë's opposition was perfectly natural. Most fathers are, whether consciously or unconsciously, jealous of any man who wishes to marry their daughter, and Mr Brontë was a tired old man, unwilling or unable to suffer any more losses or endure any changes. In the event, though he was to lose Charlotte, his life changed very little as Mr Nicholls looked after him faithfully until the end of his days. Indeed there are many ways in which Mr Nicholls was a much more convenient and comfortable son-in-law than Mr Taylor who might have taken Charlotte off to India.

Mr Taylor appears to have got on well with Mr Brontë, although we do not know how much Charlotte told her father about Mr Taylor's matrimonial intentions. Mr Taylor came from the sophisticated world of London, whereas Mr Nicholls came from the simple world of Ireland which Mr Brontë had learned to despise. Here again Mr Brontë's fears were unjustified, since Mr Nicholls's home in Ireland, to which he eventually retired, seems to have been a great deal grander than that of Mr Brontë, and the latter's snobbery, as well as being worthless, also appears to have been groundless.

Mr Nicholls and Mr Brontë should have been united by their common profession. In *The Last Chronicle of Barset*, when Archdeacon Grantley's son wished to marry Josiah Crawley's daughter, the two clergymen can reconcile the immense gap between them in wealth and social distinction by the comforting thought that they are both gentlemen. Mr Nicholls's Anglo-Catholicism, fashionable at the time, may have seemed opposed to Mr Brontë's old-fashioned Evangelicalanism, but doctrinal differences can hardly have caused all that much difficulty, since the two men had worked together without strain for seven years. On the issue of berating the Nonconformists, it was Charlotte rather than Mr Brontë who found fault with Mr Nicholls's vigour, since Mr Brontë's Toryism and his support for Church rates had led him to oppose the Nonconformists in the past.

Neither Mr Brontë nor Mr Nicholls were quite as gentlemanly as Mr Crawley and Archdeacon Grantley, and it is likely that one accusation which Mr Brontë may have levelled against Mr Nicholls is that he was trying to marry Charlotte for her money. Charlotte hints at this on 18 December 1852.[5] This accusation was probably unjust, although Charlotte had in six difficult years earned fifteen hundred pounds, and gave every assurance of continuing to provide this tidy income. Mr Brontë may have felt that Mr Nicholls was unworthy of Charlotte, and here the modern reader may have more sympathy with the older man.

Charlotte's heroes tend to be men of strong character, keen intelligence and sincere beliefs. Mr Nicholls does not seem to have lived up to these ideals; his dog-like devotion to Charlotte, and then to her father after Charlotte's death, though admirable, hardly appear quite so exciting. When Mr Brontë died, he retired to Ireland,

married his cousin, and apparently ceased to practice as a clergyman; this does not seem very like the conduct of Mr Rochester or St
John Rivers. He defended Charlotte's memory with more vigour
than tact in the Cowan Bridge controversy, helped edit *The Professor*
with some rather peculiar pieces of censorship, took the juvenilia
with him to Ireland, where he occasionally copied a poem, and was
eventually, admittedly in his old age, swindled by Shorter and Wise
into parting with them for money. His dealings with Ellen Nussey,
not herself the eaiest and most sensible of people, were embarassing
in Charlotte's lifetime, and in later life when it came to publishing
the letters, brought credit to neither party and infinite difficulties to
any student of the Brontës.

This is not a good record, although Mr Nicholls was no doubt a
good man after his lights; there is oral tradition of his kindness to
people in Haworth. But Charlotte did not love him. She says so in
her first letter to Ellen Nussey. How and why she changed her mind
is hard to determine in view of the missing evidence. Initially we
hear a good deal of Mr Nicholls, but, though Charlotte says she
pities him, there is much else in these early letters which suggests
that she was very far from overcoming her initial antipathy. She says
in the revealing letter of 18 December that her father thought Mr
Nicholls had behaved with disingenuousness in concealing his aim.
She declares this is not altogether groundless, but that her own
objections arise from a sense of incongruity and uncongeniality in
feelings, taste and ideals.

Mr Nicholls tried to resign, but Mr Brontë said he would only let
him go on condition that he would promise never to mention the
matter of the marriage again. The two men neither met nor spoke,
but communicated by letter. It must have been embarrassing for
Charlotte, and on 5 January she left for the Smiths in London,
staying there for four weeks. The publication of *Villette* on 28
January 1853 provided some distraction. After the harsh reviews of
Jane Eyre on the subject of coarseness, critics could find little to cavil
at on this score in *Villette*, and the reviews were generally
favourable. Charlotte was however sorely wounded by a review in
the *Daily News* and a letter from Harriet Martineau, the author of the
review, complaining that there was too much love in the novel. The
criticism must have seemed sadly ironic for Charlotte, still wrestling
with Mr Nicholls's proposal, but she was pleased by the way her
book had been received, and wrote to Mrs Gaskell a cheerful letter
on 24 February, comparing the winter that had just passed very

favourably with her sickness and sorrow in the previous winter.[6]

Mr Nicholls had been faring less well. On 4 March Charlotte wrote to Ellen Nussey about the visit of the Bishop. The Bishop of Ripon, Charles Longley, who was later to become Archbishop of York and then of Canterbury, behaved very well, but Mr Nicholls demeaned himself less pleasantly, appearing dejected before the Bishop, showing bad temper to Mr Brontë, following Charlotte up the lane, and involving himself in a dispute with the inspector – presumably the inspector of Church Schools. Charlotte wished he would go away. Later the Bishop spoke kindly of Mr Nicholls.[7]

Ellen Nussey had been concerned all winter as to whether she should take a job as a companion to the wife of a clergyman in Norfolk, a Mrs Upjohn. Like Charlotte, Ellen was reaching the age when marriage prospects were receding, and she had no literary resources to help her. This fact must have made her jealous of Charlotte's suitor, even though Charlotte spoke so ill of Mr Nicholls, pitying him but complaining of his dreary gloom in a letter of 6 April. She also complained of her father's bitter and unreasonable prejudices, but said she would not oppose them.[8]

At the end of April Charlotte left home, going first to Mrs Gaskell's in Manchester, then to Ellen Nussey. When she returned she found Mr Nicholls was about to leave. His behaviour, faltering on Whit Sunday in the middle of the service, refusing to speak to Mr Brontë, bursting into a paroxysm of tears on his final departure aroused pity in Charlotte and contempt in her father. In June Charlotte fell severely ill with influenza and had to postpone a visit from Mrs Gaskell. Mr Brontë also became ill with a threatened return of blindness, and the summer cannot have been happy one for either of the inhabitants of Haworth Parsonage. Charlotte relieved her feelings by writing a letter to the editor of *The Christian Remembrancer* a periodical which had given a hostile review of *Villette*. In it she explained with dignity her reasons for seclusion from the world.

This seclusion was broken by a short visit to Scotland in August and to Yorkshire in the company of Joe Taylor, his wife, the former Amelia Ringrose, and their baby. The visit, described in a letter to the staid Miss Wooler,[9] does not seem to have been a success, since the baby was ill, and Charlotte thought both parents spoiled it. In September Mrs Gaskell made her postponed visit to Haworth.

First impressions are important, and much of what Mrs Gaskell felt about Haworth on her first visit found its way into her biography. She came, as visitors to Haworth should come, on a dull, drizzly day and was struck by the remoteness of Haworth, its steep main street and the grim surroundings. The loneliness of Charlotte, the eccentricity of her father, and her devotion to her sisters all colour Mrs Gaskell's account. Visits to the moors and, a surprising touch, Charlotte's calls on rough cottages where she received a warm welcome are mentioned. Mrs Gaskell, a kindly and sympathetic woman, had a novelist's interest in human nature and a novelist's eye for detail. Her admiration for Charlotte's fortitude is plain, but she perhaps exaggerated Charlotte's pathos at this difficult time of her life.

Clearly Charlotte mentioned Mr Nicholls to Mrs Gaskell. One wonders whether Mrs Gaskell encouraged Charlotte to think more highly of him; she spoke harshly of Mr Brontë's attitude and later spoke kindly of Mr Nicholls. Mr Nicholls was at Kirk Smeaton near Pontefract from August 11, and corresponded with Charlotte. Charlotte replied to him and eventually confessed to her father the correspondence. We do not know when this confession occurred. After Mrs Gaskell left Charlotte went to stay with Miss Wooler for a week at Hornsea on the East Yorkshire coast, and in November she planned to go to London. In January Charlotte did receive a visit from Mr Nicholls who had presumably come to stay with his friend Mr Grant at Oxenhope. He was not very pleasantly received at Haworth, but the fact that he was received at all suggests that the sanctioning of the correspondence must have preceded the visit.

Most of this information comes from the letters of Charlotte to Ellen in the spring of 1854.[10] At one stage Charlotte misdirected a letter, probably intended for Mr Nicholls, to Ellen. Her eventual confession that she was engaged to him must have caused both parties some embarrassment. In February 1854 Mary Hewitt wrote to Ellen suggesting some kind of estrangement between the friends.[11] Also in February 1854, but replying to a letter of Ellen's written in August 1853, Mary Taylor seemed to think that it was quite likely that Charlotte would be married, briskly dismissing the objections of Ellen and Mr Brontë.[12]

Some more graphic and sentimental details of the courtship are supplied by Catherine Winkworth, a friend of Mrs Gaskell's, who said in a rather breathless letter of 8 May to Emma Shaen that Mr Nicholls had written six times before Charlotte had deigned to answer, and then only to receive the answer that he must bear his lot with heroic submission.[13] There may be a certain amount of exaggeration in this letter, which does not show Charlotte in a particularly happy frame of mind. She worried about Mr Nicholls's intellectual abilities and his stiff Puseyite views. Miss Winkworth guessed that Charlotte's true love was Paul Emanuel who was dead, and she was half right.

Mr Brontë's objections to Mr Nicholls had been lessened by the discovery that he had been a very good curate, and that his substitute, Mr de Renzl, caused a great deal of trouble. Whether Mr Brontë considered his daughter's feelings on the matter is an open question; it is difficult for any of us to guess what her feelings were. Clearly the threat of loneliness played a part. Mr Brontë could not live forever, and when he died Charlotte would have nobody to talk to, and no home to fall back on. Had Charlotte lived, Mr Nicholls would have been Mr Brontë's natural successor.

All this seems very unromantic to us and, no doubt, seemed unromantic to Charlotte. Another motive may be considered. Throughout 1853 and the first part of 1854 we hear very little of literature. She did correspond with George Smith and W. S. Williams over the reviews of *Villette*, but the correspondence seems to have died down in the summer of 1853.[14] She thanks Williams for a box of books for the last time on 6 December. In congratulating George Smith on his marriage on 25 April 1854, only after he had written to her about hers, she says how distant Cornhill seems.[15] Although *Villette* had been finished on 20 November 1852 there is no mention of any future book in any letter of the next two years. *Emma* was begun in November 1853 but little progress was made. Charlotte's visit to Miss Wooler in October was probably in search of material, as *Emma* is about a school. The projected visit to London in November may have been with the same object. But the book did not advance very far, and Miss Wooler was one of the people Charlotte consulted about Mr Nicholls.

Charlotte had faced considerable distress in writing *Villette*. She appeared pleased by reviews, but some had hurt her. Writing another book, far from being a solace against the pangs of loneliness, may have seemed likely to make them more bitter. *Villette* had drained Charlotte emotionally and physically, and the tactlessly timed proposal of Mr Nicholls at first sight may have seemed – as it still seems to us – an almost comic intrusion of reality into the poignant world of the imagination. As 1853 progressed, the world of the imagination no longer seemed to be so powerful. The humdrum world of clerical chit-chat, tea parties and sermons, parish visiting and Sunday Schools, against which Charlotte had spoken so bitterly in *Shirley*, may have seemed a safe haven after *Villette*. In the latter novel reason and imagination had fought many a bitter battle, and as summer wore on into autumn and winter they no doubt fought the same battle in Charlotte's mind as Mr Nicholls doggedly persisted in his suit.

Eventually reason won, Mr Brontë's resistance crumbled, and Charlotte announced her engagement in a letter to Ellen on 11 April 1854. Mr Nicholls, having gained his point, relapsed unromantically into rheumatism or hypochondria, and Mr Brontë fell ill. Charlotte soberly prepared for a quiet wedding. Cards were sent to people like George Smith and Mrs Gaskell, but of course they were not expected to come, and did not. Only Ellen Nussey and Miss Wooler attended the wedding with the latter improbably stepping in for Mr Brontë as the person who gave the bride away.

The wedding took place on 29 June. On the same evening Charlotte wrote from Conway to Ellen Nussey.[16] The letter was mainly about the weather. Reason had finally won over imagination. Other letters on the honeymoon in Ireland are, as one would expect, happy, although there are ominous signs of ill health. Charlotte was pleased at the prosperity of Mr Nicholls's family and the fact that he allowed her to indulge her romantic fantasies on the Atlantic coast. The honeymoon tour seems to have been well planned, although perhaps a little too hectic.

When she arrived back at Haworth Charlotte wrote on 9 August 1854 a slightly strained letter to Ellen Nussey. She complains of being too busy, saying 'to be constantly called for and occupied seems so strange yet it is a marvellously good thing'. She concludes with a slightly more pessimistic paragraph.

> Dear Nell – during the last six weeks – the colour of my thoughts is a good deal changed: I know more of the realities of life than once I did. I think many false ideas are propagated perhaps unintentionally. I think those married women who indiscriminately urge their acquaintance to marry – much to blame. For my part – I can only say with deeper sincerity and further significance – what I always said in theory – wait God's will. Indeed – indeed Nell – it is a solemn and strange and perilous thing for a woman to become a wife. Man's lot is far – far different.[17]

There are possibly some veiled references to the secrets of the marriage bed, not probably grasped by Ellen Nussey. We are again here aware how far Charlotte is removed in these short sentences from the world of the novels, where women and men seem equally keen to marry. To Miss Wooler Charlotte is more circumspect, although she does say that Mr Nicholls took up a great deal of her time, and the sentences describing the parish welcome on their return have a tired and insincere air. 'They seemed to enjoy it much, and it was pleasant to see their happiness'.[18]

Ellen visited Haworth in October. There may have been a plan to marry her off to one of the two Sowden brothers, clerical acquaintances of Mr Nicholls. In October an awkward quarrel arose over whether Ellen Nussey should preserve Charlotte's correspondence. Mr Nicholls read Charlotte's letters, pronounced them rash and said Ellen must promise to destroy them, or he would act as a censor to the correspondence. Ellen agreed on condition that Mr Nicholls pledged himself to no authorship in the matter communicated. Charlotte wrote that Arthur thanked Ellen for her pledge. Ellen censored this remark, but said in a postscript to the note she had written that as Mr Nicholls continued his censorship, the pledge was void.[19]

It is difficult, as one reads Charlotte's embarrassed attempts to keep the peace between her friend and her husband, to avoid feeling impatience with both Ellen Nussey and Mr Nicholls. Ellen seems to have been both tactless and dishonest, Mr Nicholls selfish and overbearing. Fortunately the latent hostility between the two was kept in control during Charlotte's lifetime, but one wonders what possibility Charlotte would have had of a literary career with Mr Nicholls in control. Later he denied that he had interfered with Charlotte's writing, but the evidence of the letters which Charlotte wrote to Ellen Nussey makes his statement unconvincing.

Sir James Kay Shuttleworth paid a visit to Haworth in November and offered Mr Nicholls the living at Padiham near his home at Ganthorpe. Mr Nicholls was obliged to refuse, since he had to stay at Haworth as long as Mr Brontë was alive. Mr Nicholls suggested Mr Sowden, and Charlotte eagerly reported this to Ellen Nussey, but nothing came of the matter. The friend of Charlotte Brontë's husband was hardly the same as the husband himself, but Charlotte seemed blind to the fact that she was the real cause of Mr Nicholls's attractiveness to Sir James.

On 29 November Charlotte was about to write to Ellen Nussey when Mr Nicholls asked her to come for a walk. They went as far as the waterfall and were caught in a storm. On 7 December Charlotte said she had caught a cold as a result of this escapade, and postponed a visit to Brookroyd until after Christmas.[20] She again complained of being perpetually busy: there was no time to read the French papers. Writing on 28 December to Ellen's sister she said she was unlikely to get off to Brookroyd, since there were cases where wives had just to put their own judgement on the shelf and do as they were bid. It is true that on 26 December Charlotte called Mr Nicholls her 'dear boy', dearer now than he was six months ago. Ellen, annoyed at the interference of Mr Nicholls, was later to use the episode of the waterfall as an example of his inhumanity, and Haworth folklore to this day still spins stories about Mr Nicholls as a kind of Heathcliff-like ogre who dragged his ailing wife out on the moors to her death.

Such a story is certainly unjust. There is no further mention of ill health in the letters of December, in which Charlotte's principal concern seemed to be the health of Joe Taylor at Hunsworth. On 19 January 1854 Charlotte said she had been quite well since her return from Ireland until about ten days before when her stomach had seemed to lose its tone.[21] The symptoms Charlotte describes resemble those of morning sickness, but Charlotte told Ellen not to conjecture, as it was too soon to do so. The next four letters to Ellen come from Mr Nicholls; they neither confirm nor deny any suggestion of pregnancy. In February Charlotte wrote two letters to Ellen and two to Amelia Taylor praising her husband's devotion as a nurse, and complaining of 'terrible sickness all night' and of herself being reduced to a skeleton. On 31 March Mr Nicholls reported the melancholy news to Ellen that Charlotte had died of exhaustion the previous night.[22]

The death certificate gives the cause of death as phthisis, i.e. tuberculosis. There is nothing apart from Charlotte's initial symptoms to suggest pregnancy, although she did make provision for children in her will, and did consult Amelia Taylor, herself fairly recently a mother, about possible medicines. Charlotte's unborn child has entered Haworth folklore, but like most Brontë legends has little evidence to support it. It is fascinating to speculate on what the fate of such a child would have been; the only child of the Brownings is perhaps a warning against expecting too much.

It is equally fascinating to speculate on what Charlotte's life would have been like if she had lived. We have seen how Mr Nicholls encroached upon her time and her writing. Conflicts between duty and inclination loom large in Charlotte's novels, but we find it hard to imagine that her duty towards her husband and her father would not have prevailed. If there had been any children the inclination to write would have had even less claim. Nor is there much evidence to show that Charlotte had much inclination to write in the last two years of her life. She might, had she lived, have been prevailed upon to write another novel as a duty to her public and to her family; such a novel would have scarcely been likely to have been such a success as the other novels, forged with difficulty in lonely hours as an antidote to disappointment and despair.

The story of the other main actors in this chapter can, as in the last chapter of one of Charlotte's novels, be briefly told. Mr Brontë survived his daughter by six years, loyally tended by Mr Nicholls whose dogged devotion to his wife's father and his wife's reputation cannot be denied. They did not earn him much reward, since he was not appointed to the living at Haworth, and returned to Ireland in October 1861 taking up the unexacting life of a gentleman farmer until 1906. Ellen Nussey also survived her friend for a long time, but her old age was an unhappy one, marred by the difficulties involved in disposing of and publishing Charlotte's letters. Her quarrels with Mr Nicholls, and eventually with almost everyone concerned with the Brontës, provide a sad, sour postscript to the Brontë story.

Our concern must be with Charlotte. Perhaps she was lucky to die when she did, secure in her reputation as an author and secure in the love of her husband. The next ten years might have eroded this security. Like all Brontë biographers I feel protective towards Charlotte. In spite or because of her faults, her prickly vulnerability, her purblind romanticism, her startling insensitivity, her intolerance, her dogmatism and her unkindness Charlotte Brontë is a deeply sympathetic character. Her courage, her sincerity, her devotion to the truth, her high-mindedness in moral and intellectual matters shine forth in her life and in her books even in an age which has lost its bearings. Upright, forthright and downright, Charlotte Brontë is a good guardian angel against silliness and sin.

Notes

Manuscripts have been consulted wherever possible, and the library where the manuscript is, is shown in parenthesis after the Shakespeare Head reference. Where no manuscript is available the Shakespeare Head version is given and the reference has no parenthesis. With recent acquisitions by the Brontë Society the number of letters printed in the Shakespeare Head version for which there is no manuscript is now surprisingly small, although there are several letters for which we have manuscripts, and there is no version in the Shakespeare Head. Some caution must be exercised with dates, as on several occasions the date given in the Shakespeare Head is a conjectural one.

For an explanation of the abbreviations used in the notes see p. ix.

NOTES TO THE INTRODUCTION

1. V. Moore, *The Life and Eager Death of Emily Brontë* (London, 1936).
2. There is an account of some modern Brontë criticism by K. Blake, 'Review of Brontë Studies, 1975–80', in *Dickens Studies Annual*, 10 (1982) pp. 221–40.
3. J. Chapple and A. Pollard (eds), *The Letters of Mrs Gaskell* (Manchester, 1966) pp. 168–9.
4. For this hostility, the roots of which lie in the history of the last two years of Charlotte's life, see CW, pp. 128–37.
5. Sir C. Tennyson, *Alfred Tennyson* (London, 1950).

NOTES TO CHAPTER 1: ORIGINS

1. E. Chitham, *The Brontës' Irish Background* (London, 1986).
2. Mrs Ward's preface to the Haworth edition of *Wuthering Heights* (London, 1899) stressing the Brontës' Celtic origins clearly owes much to her uncle's earlier vague racist theories, notably those expressed in M. Arnold, *On the Study of Celtic Literature* (London, 1867).
3. Chitham, *The Brontës' Irish Background*, pp. 32–63.
4. D. Newsome, *The Parting of Friends* (London, 1966) gives the best explanation of this phenomenon.
5. SHLL, I, pp. 213–14 (BCH); 214–15 (HLC). The impression we form from these letters is that Charlotte disliked her cousins for the grand airs they gave themselves. SHLL, III, pp. 280–1 (FWM), p. 282 tell us

of the later visit. Charlotte wrote two letters to her cousin Eliza Kingston about railway shares in 1846 (BCNY and BPM).

6. J. Horsfall Turner (ed.), *The Reverend Patrick Brontë, A.B.: His Collected Works and Life* (Bingley, 1898).

7. The diary is to be found in Sheffield University Library. Extracts are in SHLL, I, pp. 39–45.

8. SHLL, I, pp. 121–2, 145–6, 214–15 (all in HLC). When Charlotte became famous Amelia tried to trade on her acquaintance, as we see from SHLL, III, pp. 204–5 (BPM), 223–4 (BCH).

9. Books on Mr Brontë, such as A. Hopkins, *Father of the Brontës* (Baltimore, 1958) and J. Lock and W. Dixon, *A Man of Sorrow: The Life, Letters and Times of the Rev. Patrick Brontë* (London, 1965), are generally favourable to their subject, but a number of modern Brontë biographers have cast aspersions on him. Neither Mrs Gaskell nor Charlotte's two friends Ellen Nussey and Mary Taylor were fond of Charlotte's father; this may be evidence against him, but it must also be a fact to bear in mind when weighing the evidence.

NOTES TO CHAPTER 2: PUPIL

1. SHLL, I, pp. 202–3 (HLC).

2. CW, pp. 78–9.

3. This association of Miss Branwell with Calvinism has a long history, but is quite unjustified. It springs partly from a good deal of confusion about just what was involved in Calvinism. Belief in eternal damnation, common to most religious sects, is something different from belief in preordination to damnation. The Brontës at times had fears about the latter, but eventually in unorthodox fashion rebelled against the former (see *BB*, pp. 28–47).

4. SHLL, II, pp. 173–4 (HLC). The index in the Shakespeare Head Edition, normally very reliable, is defective on Cowan Bridge, although there is a valuable appendix about the controversy after Charlotte's death.

5. M. Curtis, 'Cowan Bridge School: An Old Prospectus Reexamined', *BST*, 63 (1953) pp. 187–92, and B. Harrison, 'The Real Miss Temple', *BST*, 85 (1975) pp. 361–4 clear up some wild speculation.

6. Extracts from *Youthful Memoirs*, *The Children's Friend* and *First Tales* are published in SHLL, I, pp. 69–73, and they do not appear unrepresentative selections.

7. C. Shepheard-Walwyn, *Henry and Margaret Jane Shepheard; Memorials of a Father and Mother* (London, 1882).

8. SHLL, IV, pp. 85–7; II, pp. 150–1; I, pp. 89–92.

9. W. Gerin, *Branwell Brontë* (London, 1961) pp. 12–16, 114–19.

10. J. Stevens (ed.), *Mary Taylor, Friend of Charlotte Brontë: Letters from New Zealand and Elsewhere* (Oxford, 1972) illustrates this clearly.

11. CW, pp. 131–7.

12. SHLL, I, pp. 142–3 (HLC). See Chapter 5. J. Maynard, *Charlotte Brontë and Sexuality* (Cambridge, 1984) delves into this problem, not very sensitively.

NOTES TO CHAPTER 3: WRITER

1. This chapter is heavily indebted to C. Alexander, *The Early Writings of Charlotte Brontë* (London 1983). The forthcoming edition of the juvenilia will no doubt make the issue of the juvenilia clearer, in particular helping to settle the question of their literary merit.
2. Alexander, *The Early Writings of Charlotte Brontë*, p. 25.
3. CW, pp. 78–9.
4. W. Gerin, *Charlotte Brontë: The Evolution of Genius* (Oxford, 1966) pp. 87–92 exaggerates the division between the brother and sister, and in general Branwell's prose writings, still to be deciphered, have had a poor press, although his poetry is better than that of Charlotte.
5. SHCP, p. 134. This is often seen as an effort to escape from the Glass Town Saga, but if so it was not a very wholehearted one.
6. CW, p. 129.
7. SHLL, I, pp. 118, 119–20 (HLC).
8. SHLL, I, pp. 126–7.
9. *Memoirs of Harriette Wilson, Written by Herself* was published in 1825, but we have no indication of how Charlotte might have read it.
10. SHCP, p. 233.

NOTES TO CHAPTER 4: TEACHER

1. CW, pp. 130–1.
2. SHLL, I, pp. 130–1 (BPM).
3. CW, pp. 20–33.
4. SHLL, I, p. 142 (HLC).
5. For the chronology of this period see SHBP, pp. xx–xxi.
6. BB, pp. 19–21.
7. SHCP, p. 204.
8. SHLL, I, pp. 129–30 (HLC), 143–4, 163–4 (BCH), 165–6 (BCH). The years of some of these letters are still conjectural, but the length of the holidays seems established.
9. Alexander, *The Early Writings of Charlotte Brontë*, p. 154.
10. Gerin, *Charlotte Brontë*, pp. 109–11.
11. Ibid., p. 125.
12. SHLL, I, pp. 183–5 (HLC), 196–7 (PML). Even the name of this suitor is obscure. The manuscripts of both letters clearly say Price, but Pryce appears on the death certificate. Bryce seems an error which has gained authority by repetition.
13. Gerin, *Charlotte Brontë*, pp. 149–50.
14. A. C. Benson, *The Life of Edward Benson, Sometime Archbishop of Canterbury* (London, 1899) I, p. 12.
15. G, p. 172.

NOTES TO CHAPTER 5: BELGIUM

1.   G. Holderness, *Wuthering Heights* (Milton Keynes, 1985) p. 75.
2.   G, pp. 15–35; SHLL, I, pp. 151–2, 185–2 (BPM), 202–3 (HLC).
3.   SHLL, I, pp. 193–4 (HLC).
4.   Alexander, *The Early Writings of Charlotte Brontë*, pp. 204–9 gives a good summary of *Ashworth*, which is also the subject of a Ph.D. dissertation by Melodie Monahan at the University of Rochester in 1976.
5.   SHCP, pp. 231–3, 54–6.
6.   Alexander, *The Early Writings of Charlotte Brontë*, p. 288.
7.   Gerin, *Branwell Brontë*, p. 175.
8.   SHLL, I, pp. 194–5.
9.   The letter is printed in full in *The Times Literary Supplement* of 14 May 1970.
10. See Stevens (ed.), *Mary Taylor*, pp. 16–17. SHLL, I, pp. 284–5 (HLC) shows a possible romance of Ellen with the Taylor brothers.
11. *BB*, p. 20.
12. SHLL, I, pp. 249–50 (HLC).
13. SHLL, I, pp. 230–1.
14. *BB*, p. 98.
15. Gerin, *Charlotte Brontë*, pp. 189–94.
16. SHLL, I, pp. 258 (PML), 259–61, 266–7 (HLC).
17. SHLL, I, pp. 259–61.
18. E. Duthie, *The Foreign Vision of Charlotte Brontë* (London, 1975) gives a good account of these exercises, some of which are translated in *BST*, 62 (1952) pp. 88–99; 64 (1954) pp. 273–85; and 65 (1955) pp. 361–85.
19. SHLL, I, pp. 278–81, 308–9 (PML).
20. Gerin, *Branwell Brontë*, pp. 214–15.
21. SHLL, I, p. 282 (FWM), 284 (HUL).
22. SHLL, I, pp. 293–4 (BPM). Printed in full in *BST*, 90 (1980) pp. 356–8.
23. SHLL, I, pp. 306–7 (HLC).
24. SHLL, I, pp. 303–4.
25. Gerin, *Charlotte Brontë*, p. 247 (BPM).
26. Duthie, *The Foreign Vision of Charlotte Brontë*, pp. 46–56.
27. PUL.

NOTES TO CHAPTER 6: AUTHOR

1.   HRT.
2.   SHLL, II, pp. 9–14 (BL).
3.   This is the main thrust of Duthie's valuable book, *The Foreign Vision of Charlotte Brontë*, especially shown in pp. 20–60.
4.   SHCP, pp. 244, 336.
5.   SHCP, pp. 24, 243.
6.   SHLL, II, pp. 114–15 (HLC).

7. CW, pp. 1–13.
8. SHLL, II, pp. 27–9.
9. SHLL, II, pp. 39–30 (HLC).
10. SHLL, II, pp. 17–19 (BL), pp. 52–53 (BPM).
11. Gerin, *Branwell Brontë*, pp. 240–2.
12. SHLL, II, pp. 96–7 (BPM). Printed in full in *BST*, 90 (1980) pp. 356–8.
13. This is to be found in her biographical notice in the Second Edition of *Wuthering Heights*.
14. The three sisters had their poems printed in such a way that one of Anne's followed one of Emily's which followed one of Charlotte's.
15. SHLL, II, pp. 76–7.
16. D. Roper, 'The Revision of Emily Brontë's Poems', *The Library*, 6.6 (1984) pp. 153–67.
17. All the Brontës were poor spellers, especially Emily. See C. Hatfield (ed.), *The Complete Poems of Emily Jane Brontë* (Oxford, 1941) pp. 22–3.
18. SHCP, p. 44.
19. SHCP, p. 16.
20. SHCP, p. 62.
21. SHLL, II, pp. 254–6 (BL).
22. Preface to the Second Edition of *Wuthering Heights*.
23. SHLL, II, p. 136 (BCH).

NOTES TO CHAPTER 7: *JANE EYRE*

1. G, p. 314.
2. SHLL, II, pp. 117–18 (HLC), 126–7.
3. G, p. 313.
4. SHLL, II, pp. 261–2, (PML), but this may involve wishful thinking on Charlotte's part.
5. CW, pp. 84–90.
6. Gerin, *Charlotte Brontë*, p. 202.
7. SHLL, II, pp. 114–15 (HLC), 118–19 (HLC), 121–2, 126–7.
8. SHLL, II, pp. 140–2 (BPM). Some additional letters are printed by A. Pollard in 'The Seton-Gordon–Brontë Letters', *BST*, 92 (1982) pp. 101–14.
9. Preface to the Second Edition of *Wuthering Heights*.
10. Gerin, *Charlotte Brontë*, p. 336.
11. G. Haight, *George Eliot* (London, 1967) p. 268.
12. SHLL, II, p. 175 (BPM), incorrectly dated in SHLL (see *BST*, 63 (1953) pp. 194–5) pp. 211–25, 226–8 (HLC).
13. SHLL, II, pp. 142, 143, 149 (BPM).
14. *BB*, pp. 115–16.
15. SHLL, II, pp. 177–8.
16. SHLL, II, pp. 152–3 (BL).
17. SHLL, II, pp. 192–3, 196–7 (HLC).
18. SHLL, II, pp. 161–2 (PUL).

19. I. Holgate, 'The Structure of *Shirley*', *BST*, 72 (1962) pp. 28–9, although doubt is cast on this by H. Rosengarten and M. Smith (ed.), *Shirley* (Oxford, 1979) p. xvi.
20. SHLL, II, pp. 289–291 (BPM).
21. J. Stevens (ed.), *Mary Taylor* pp. 5–9 shows the links between the Yorkes and the Taylors.
22. Stevens, *Mary Taylor*, pp. 176–81 gives the full text. SHLL, II, pp. 250–4 is defective.
23. SHLL, II, pp. 246–7 (BPM), 247–50 (FWM).
24. SHLL, II, pp. 254–6 (BL).
25. *BB*, pp. 28–47.
26. SHLL, II, pp. 267–8, 270–1, 288 (BPM). Full text in *BST*, 90 (1980) pp. 359–60.
27. SHLL, II, pp. 293, 294 (BCNY).
28. W. Gerin, *Emily Brontë* (Oxford, 1971) pp. 246–7.
29. P. Drew, 'Charlotte Brontë as a Critic of *Wuthering Heights*', *Nineteenth-Century Fiction*, 18 (1963–4) pp. 365–81.
30. SHCP, pp. xviii, 241.

NOTES TO CHAPTER 8: *SHIRLEY*

1. SHLL, II, pp. 306–7 (BPM). For details of the composition and publication of *Shirley* the introduction to the Clarendon Edition, ed. H. Rosengarten and M. Smith (Oxford, 1979), is invaluable.
2. SHLL, II, pp. 325–7 (PUL).
3. SHLL, II, pp. 328–30.
4. G, pp. 404–8.
5. SHLL, II, pp. 347–8, 348–9 (BPM).
6. Charlotte on 30 October 1852 in a letter to George Smith said that she had been able to discuss the first two volumes of *Shirley* with someone else in contrast to *Villette*, which she had written all by herself. See SHLL, IV, pp. 13–14 (BPM).
7. SHLL, III, p. 15.
8. SHLL, III, pp. 7–8, 9 (BCH).
9. SHLL, III, pp. 11–12 (BPM).
10. For this and other reviews of *Shirley*, see *BB*, pp. 123–8.
11. SHLL, III, p. 12 (BCL), pp. 13–14 (BCH).
12. The preface is printed in *BST*, 85 (1975), and in the Clarendon Edition of *Shirley*, pp. 801–4. On 4 September Charlotte refused to write another preface, but did cancel some allusions to *The Quarterly* in *Shirley*: for her revisions of the text see the Clarendon *Shirley*, pp. xxiii, 425, 640.
13. SHLL, III, pp. 17 (BCH), 21 (BCH), 23 (BPM).
14. SHLL, III, pp. 23–4 (BPM), 36–7.
15. SHLL, III, pp. 36–7.
16. The classic article on the biographical background of Shirley is I. Holgate, 'The Structure of *Shirley*', *BST*, 72 (1962) pp. 7–35.

17. There has not been much critical attention paid to *Shirley*. J. Korg, 'The Problem of Unity in *Shirley*', *Nineteenth-Century Fiction*, 12 (1957–8) 125–36, and A. Shapiro, 'Public Themes and Private Lives: Social Criticism in *Shirley*', *Papers on Language and Literature*, 4 (1968) pp. 74–84 deal with the objection that the novel is too widely diffused.
18. Oscar Wilde, *The Importance of Being Earnest* (London, 1985) Act I.
19. SHLL, III, p. 234 (HRT).
20. SHLL, III, p. 31 (BL).
21. *BB*, pp. 124–5.
22. *BB*, p. 127.
23. SHLL, III, p. 59 (BPM).
24. SHLL, III, pp. 69, 73 (BCNY).
25. SHLL, III, p. 55.
26. SHLL, III, pp. 135–6 (BCNY).
27. SHLL, III, pp. 104–6 (BPM).
28. SHLL, III, pp. 212–13 (BCNY).

NOTES TO CHAPTER 9: *VILLETTE*

1. SHLL, IV, pp. 22–3 (BPM). Text incorrectly printed. The character of Paulina is presumably that described as both the weakest and the most beautiful.
2. SHLL, III, p. 43 (PML).
3. SHLL, III, p. 55 (BCNY).
4. SHLL, III, p. 634 (BPM).
5. SHLL, III, pp. 130, (BPM), 131–2 (BPM), 130–2 (BPM); the dates are not certain.
6. SHLL, III, pp. 140–6 (BCL).
7. SHLL, III, pp. 153–5 (HRT), 156–7 (PML), 161–2, 165 (HUL).
8. SHLL, III, pp. 166 (BCH), 166–7 (HLC), 173–4 (HLC).
9. SHLL, III, pp. 175–7 (BDM), 177–9 (HRT).
10. SHLL, III, p. 189 (HLC).
11. SHLL, III, pp. 192–3 (HRT), 194–7 (BPM), 199–201, (HRT), 201–2, 204–5 (BPM).
12. SHLL, III, pp. 206 (HLC), 206–7 (BPM).
13. M. M. Brammer, 'The Manuscript of *The Professor*', *Review of English Studies*, 11 (1960) p. 157.
14. SHLL, III, p. 208 (HRT).
15. SHLL, III, pp. 210–11 (BPM).
16. SHLL, III, pp. 220–1 (BPM), 222 (BPM), 223–4 (HUL).
17. SHLL, III, pp. 228–9 (BPM).
18. SHLL, III, pp. 230–1 (HLC).
19. SHLL, III, pp. 255–6, (BPM), 258–9 (BPM), 259–61 (BPM). The full text of SHLL, III, p. 271 has not been published. Extracts from it and other unpublished letters now in the BPM are published in Sir T. Lever, 'Charlotte Brontë and George Smith', in *BST*, 87 (1977)

pp. 106–14, but there is no real evidence for a love-affair in these letters or in other manuscripts not published by Lever. We do find Charlotte rather comically telling Smith about the rule that i precedes e except after c in an unpublished fragment of a letter of 4 August 1851 (SHLL, III, 266–7).

20. SHLL, III, pp. 288–90 (HRT).
21. SHLL, III, pp. 293–4 (BPM), 294–6 (BPM).
22. For an account of this novel see Sir T. Lever, 'Harriet Martineau and Her Novel *Oliver Weld*' in *BST*, 84 (1974) pp. 270–3.
23. SHLL, III, pp. 300 (HLC), 306 (BCH), 308–9 (FWM).
24. SHLL, III, p. 312.
25. SHLL, III, pp. 323–4 (FWM), 324 (BPM).
26. SHLL, III, p. 319 (HLC), wrongly dated by Charlotte.
27. SHLL, III, pp. 336–7 (HLC). It is possible that Mrs Smith of whom Charlotte speaks rather bafflingly in a letter at the end of 1852 as a friend whose kindness had once meant a great deal may have been worried by the closeness of her son to Charlotte Brontë and that Charlotte, realising this, wanted to keep away from the south of England.
28. SHLL, IV, pp. 5–6 (HEH).
29. SHLL, IV, pp. 16–17 (BPM).
30. SHLL, IV, pp. 17–18 (BPM).
31. SHLL, IV, pp. 20–1 (BPM).
32. SHLL, IV, pp. 22–3 (BPM, text printed with omissions), 23–4 (FWM), 24–5.
33. C. Lemon, 'The Origins of Ginevra Fanshawe', *BST*, 81 (1971) p. 51.

NOTES TO CHAPTER 10: WIFE

1. *Emma* was first published in the *Cornhill Magazine*, April 1860, and is most conveniently to be found in the same volume as *The Professor* of the Haworth Edition, ed. Mrs H. Ward and C. Shorter (London, 1899–1900).
2. Gerin, *Charlotte Brontë*, pp. 579–81.
3. BB, pp. 7–8.
4. SHLL, II, pp. 100–1 (BPM).
5. SHLL, IV, pp. 30–1 (BCNY). Some unpublished letters of March 1853 in BPM do not refer to Mr Nicholls.
6. SHLL, IV, p. 48.
7. SHLL, IV, pp. 49–50 (BPM), 113–14 (FWM).
8. SHLL, IV, pp. 56–7 (BPM).
9. SHLL, IV, pp. 81–3 (FWM).
10. SHLL, IV, pp. 110–11 (PUL), 111, 112–13 (HUL).
11. SHLL, IV, pp. 103–4.
12. SHLL, IV, pp. 104–6 (BL).
13. SHLL, IV, pp. 121–5.
14. SHLL, IV, p. 100.

15.   SHLL, IV, pp. 118–19 (BPM). Letters recently published by A. Pollard 'The Seton-Gordon–Brontë letters', *BST*, 92 (1982) pp. 101–14 show Charlotte laconically congratulating Smith on his engagement on 10 December 1853, and discussing financial arrangements on 18 April 1854. In the summer of 1853 Smith had been ill. Charlotte wrote solicitously to him, but said that their correspondence might have to die a natural death. This remark is in an unpublished part of the letter of 3 July 1853 (SHLL, IV, pp. 75–6). Charlotte did write to Smith after this letter.
16.   SHLL, IV, pp. 133–4 (BCNY).
17.   SHLL, IV, pp. 145–6.
18.   SHLL, IV, pp. 148–9 (FWM).
19.   SHLL, IV, pp. 156–7 (BDM), 157 (HRT), 157–8 (PML, text incorrectly printed).
20.   SHLL, IV, pp. 161–2 (BCNY), 164–5 (BPM).
21.   SHLL, IV, pp. 170–1 (BPM).
22.   SHLL, IV, pp. 173–8 (mostly in BPM).

Select Bibliography

Allott, M., 'Wuthering Heights: The Rejection of Heathcliff?', Essays in Criticism, 8 (1958) pp. 27–47.

——, Emily Brontë: Wuthering Heights, Casebook Series (London, 1970).

——, Charlotte Brontë: Jane Eyre and Villette, Casebook Series (London, 1973).

——, The Brontës: The Critical Heritage (London, 1974).

——, 'The Brontës', in The English Novel: Select Bibliographical Guides, ed. by A. E. Dyson (Oxford, 1974).

Arnold, M., On the Study of Celtic Literature (London, 1867).

Alexander, C., The Early Writings of Charlotte Brontë (London, 1983).

Beer, P., 'Reader, I Married Him': A Study of the Woman Characters in Jane Austen, Charlotte Brontë, Elizabeth Gaskell and George Eliot (London, 1974).

Bellour, R., Charlotte Brontë: Patrick Branwell Brontë (Mayenne, 1972).

Benson, A. C., The Life of Edward Benson, Sometime Archbishop of Canterbury, 2 vols (London, 1899).

Bentley, P., The Brontës (London, 1947).

——, The Brontës and their World (London, 1969).

Blake, K., 'Review of Brontë Studies, 1975–80', Dickens Studies Annual, 10 (1982) pp. 221–40.

Bjork, H., The Language of Truth (Lund, 1974).

Blondel, J., Emily Brontë: Experience Spirituelle et Creation Poetique (Paris, 1955).

Bradby, G. F., The Brontës and Other Essays (Oxford, 1932).

Brammer, M. M., 'The Manuscript of The Professor', Review of English Studies, n.s. 11 (1960) pp. 157–70.

Briggs, A., 'Private and Social Themes in Shirley', Brontë Society Transactions, 68 (1958) pp. 203–19.

Brontë family, The Life and Works of Charlotte Brontë and her Sisters, Haworth edn, 7 vols, ed. Mrs H. Ward and C. K. Shorter (London, 1899–1900).

——, The Shakespeare Head Brontë, 19 vols, ed. T. J. Wise and J. A. Symington (Oxford, 1931–8).

Brontë, C., The Twelve Adventurers and Other Stories, ed. C. K. Shorter and C. W. Hatfield (London, 1925).

——, Legends of Angria: Compiled from the Early Writings of Charlotte Brontë, ed. F. E. Ratchford and W. C. de Vane (New Haven, Conn., 1933).

——, The Professor, ed. P. Bentley (London, 1954).

——, Jane Eyre, ed. Q. D. Leavis (Harmondsworth, 1966).

——, Jane Eyre, ed. J. Jack and M. Smith (Oxford, 1969).

——, Five Novelettes: Passing Events, Julia, Mina Laury, Captain Henry Hastings, Caroline Vernon, transcribed and ed. W. Gerin (London, 1971).

——, Shirley, ed. A. and J. Hook (Harmondsworth, 1974).

——, *Shirley*, ed. H. J. Rosengarten and M. Smith (Oxford, 1979).

——, *Villette*, ed. H. J. Rosengarten and M. Smith (Oxford, 1984).

——, *The Poems of Charlotte Brontë*, ed. Tom Winnifrith (London, 1984).

Brontë, E. J., *The Complete Poems of Emily Jane Brontë*, ed. C. W. Hatfield (Oxford, 1941).

Brontë, Reverend P., *The Reverend Patrick Brontë, A.B.: His Collected Works and Life*, ed. J. Horsfall Turner (Bingley, 1898).

Brontë, P. B., *The Poems of Patrick Branwell Brontë*, ed. Tom Winnifrith (London, 1983).

Burkhart, C., *Charlotte Brontë: A Psychosexual Study of Her Novels* (London, 1973).

Cecil, D., *Early Victorian Novelists: Essays in Revaluation* (London, 1934).

——, 'Fresh Thoughts on the Brontës', *Brontë Society Transactions*, 83 (1973) pp. 169–76.

Chadwick, E. A., *In the Footsteps of the Brontës* (London, 1914).

Chase, R., 'The Brontës: A Centennial Observance', *Kenyon Review*, 9 (1974) pp. 487–506.

Chitham, E., 'Almost Like Twins', *Brontë Society Transactions*, 85 (1975) pp. 365–73.

——, *The Brontës' Irish Background* (London, 1986).

——, and Winnifrith, Tom, *Brontë Facts and Brontë Problems* (London, 1983).

Christian, M., 'The Brontës', in *Victorian Fiction: A Guiide to Research*, ed. L. Stevenson (Cambridge, Mass., 1964).

Colby, R. A., '*Villette* and the Life of the Mind', *Publications of the Modern Language Association*, 85 (1960) pp. 410–19.

——, *Fiction with a Purpose: Major and Minor Nineteenth Century Novels* (London, 1967).

Craik, W. A., *The Brontë Novels* (London, 1968).

Cunningham, V. W., *Everywhere Spoken Against: Dissent in the Victorian Novel* (Oxford, 1975).

Curtis, M., 'Cowan Bridge School: An Old Prospectus Reexamined', *Brontë Society Transactions*, 63 (1953) pp. 187–92.

Dessner, L. J., *The Homely Web of Truth* (The Hague, 1975).

Drew, P., 'Charlotte Brontë as a Critic of *Wuthering Heights*', *Nineteenth-Century Fiction*, 18 (1963–4) pp. 365–81.

du Maurier, D., *The Infernal World of Branwell Brontë* (London, 1960).

Dunbar, G., 'Proper Names in *Villette*', *Nineteenth-Century Fiction*, 14 (1959–60) pp. 77–80.

Duthie, E. L., *The Foreign Vision of Charlotte Brontë* (London, 1975).

Eagleton, T., *Myths of Power: A Marxist Study of the Brontës* (London, 1975).

Ewbank, I. S., *Their Proper Sphere: A Study of the Brontë Sisters as Early Victorian Female Novelists* (London, 1966).

Foster, S., *Victorian Women's Fiction: Marriage, Freedom and the Individual* (London, 1985).

Gaskell, E. C., *The Letters of Mrs Gaskell*, ed. J. A. V. Chapple and A. E. Pollard (Manchester, 1966).

——, *The Life of Charlotte Brontë*, ed. A. Shelston (Harmondsworth, 1975).

Gerin, W., *Anne Brontë* (London, 1959; revised edn. London, 1975).

——, *Branwell Brontë* (London, 1961).

——, *Charlotte Brontë: The Evolution of Genius* (Oxford, 1966).
——, *Emily Brontë* (Oxford, 1971).
Gilbert, S. M. and Gubar, S., *The Mad Woman in the Attic: The Woman Writer and the Nineteenth Century Imagination* (Yale, 1979).
Gregor, I. (ed.), *The Brontës: A Collection of Critical Essays* (Englewood Cliffs, N.J., 1970).
Grundy, F., *Pictures of the Past* (London, 1879).
Haight, G., *George Eliot* (London, 1967).
Hanson, L. and Hanson, E. M., *The Four Brontës* (Oxford, 1949; revised edn Hamden, Conn., 1967).
Harrison, A. and Stanford, D., *Anne Brontë: Her Life and Work* (London, 1959).
Harrison, B., 'The Real Miss Temple', *Brontë Society Transactions*, 85 (1975) pp. 361–4.
Harrison, G. E., *The Clue to the Brontës* (London, 1948).
Heilman, R. B., 'Charlotte Brontë, Reason and the Moon', *Nineteenth-Century Fiction*, 14 (1959–60) pp. 283–302.
——, 'Charlotte Brontë's New Gothic', in *From Jane Austen to Joseph Conrad*, ed. R. Rathburn and M. Steinmann, Jr (Minneapolis, 1958).
Hinkley, L., *The Brontës: Charlotte and Emily* (London, 1947).
Holderness, G., *Wuthering Heights* (Milton Keynes, 1985).
Holgate, I., 'The Structure of *Shirley*', *Brontë Society Transactions*, 72 (1962) pp. 27–35.
Hopkins, A., *Elizabeth Gaskell: Her Life and Work* (London, 1952).
——, *The Father of the Brontës* (Baltimore, 1958).
Johnson, E. D. H., '"Daring the Dread Glance": Charlotte's Treatment of the Supernatural in *Villette*', *Nineteenth-Century Fiction*, 20 (1965–6) pp. 325–36.
Keefe, R., *Charlotte Brontë's World of Death* (Austin, 1979).
Kettle, A., *An Introduction to the English Novel*, vol. I (London, 1951).
Knies, E. A., *The Art of Charlotte Brontë* (Ohio, 1969).
Korg, J., 'The Problem of Unity in *Shirley*', *Nineteenth-Century Fiction*, 12 (1957–8) pp. 125–36.
Lane, M., *The Brontë Story: A Reconsideration of Mrs. Gaskell's Life of Charlotte Brontë* (London, 1953).
Langford, T., 'The Three Pictures in *Jane Eyre*', *Victorian Newsletter*, 31 (1967) pp. 47–8.
Leavis, F. R., *The Great Tradition* (London, 1948).
Lemon, C., 'The Origins of Ginevra Fanshawe', *Brontë Society Transactions*, 81 (1971) p. 51.
Lever, Sir T., 'Harriet Martineau and her Novel *Oliver Weld*', *Brontë Society Transactions*, 84 (1974) pp. 270–3.
——, 'Charlotte Brontë and George Smith', *Brontë Society Transactions*, 87 (1977) pp. 106–14.
Leyland, F., *The Brontë Family: With Special Reference to Patrick Branwell Brontë*, 2 vols (London, 1886).
Lock, J. and Dixon, W. T., *A Man of Sorrow: The Life, Letters and Times of the Rev. Patrick Brontë* (London, 1965).
Lodge, D., 'Fire and Eyre: Charlotte Brontë's War of Earthly Elements', in

The Language of Fiction: Essays in Criticism and Verbal Analysis of the English Novel (London, 1961).

Martin, R., *The Accents of Persuasion: Charlotte Brontë's Novels* (London, 1966).

Maynard, J., *Charlotte Brontë and Sexuality* (Cambridge, 1984).

Millgate, J., 'Narrative Distance in *Jane Eyre*: The Relevance of the Pictures', *Modern Language Review*, 63 (1968) pp. 315–19.

Moglen, H., *Charlotte Brontë: The Self Conceived* (New York, 1976).

Moore, V., *The Life and Eager Death of Emily Brontë* (London, 1936).

Moser, L. E., 'From Portrait to Person: A Note on the Surrealistic in *Jane Eyre*', *Nineteenth-Century Fiction*, 20 (1965–6) pp. 275–81.

Newsome, D., *The Parting of Friends* (London, 1966).

Nussey, E., 'Reminiscences of Charlotte Brontë', *Scribners Monthly*, May 1871.

Oram, E. A., 'A Brief for Miss Branwell', *Brontë Society Transactions*, 74 (1964) pp. 28–38.

Paden, W. D., *An Investigation of Gondal* (New York, 1958).

Peters, M., *Charlotte Brontë: Style in the Novel* (Wisconsin, 1973).

——, *Unquiet Soul: A Biography of Charlotte Brontë* (London, 1975).

Pinion, F. B., *A Brontë Companion* (London, 1975).

Pollard, A. E., *Charlotte Brontë*, Profiles in Literature (London, 1968).

——, 'The Seton-Gordon–Brontë Letters', *Brontë Society Transactions*, 92 (1982) pp. 101–14.

Prescott, J., '*Jane Eyre*: A Romantic Exemplum with a Difference', in *Twelve Original Essays on Great Novelists*, ed. by C. Shapiro (Detroit, 1960).

Ratchford, F. E., *The Brontës' Web of Childhood* (New York, 1941).

——, *Gondal's Queen: A Novel in Verse* (Austin, 1955).

Robinson, A. M. F., *Emily Brontë* (London, 1883).

Roper, D., 'The Revision of Emily Brontë's Poems', *The Library*, 6.6 (1984) pp. 153–67.

Rosengarten, H. J., 'The Brontës', in *Victorian Fiction: A Second Guide to Research*, ed. G. H. Ford (New York, 1878).

Scargill, M. H., 'All Passion Spent: A Revaluation of *Jane Eyre*', *University of Toronto Quarterly*, 19 (1949) pp. 120–25.

Scruton, W., 'Reminiscences of the Late Miss Ellen Nussey', *Brontë Society Transactions*, 8 (1898) pp. 23–42.

Shapiro, S., 'Public Themes and Private Lives: Social Criticism in *Shirley*', *Papers on Language and Literature*, 4 (1968) pp. 74–84.

Shepheard-Walwyn, C. C. W., *Henry and Margaret Jane Shepheard, Memorials of a Father and Mother* (London, 1882).

Sherry, N., *Charlotte and Emily Brontë* (London, 1970).

Shorter, C. K., *Charlotte Brontë and Her Circle* (London, 1896).

——, *The Brontës: Life and Letters*, 2 vols (London, 1908).

Simpson, C., *Emily Brontë* (London, 1929).

Sinclair, M., *The Three Brontës* (London, 1912).

Spark, M., and Stanford, D., *Emily Brontë* (London, 1953).

Spens, J., 'Charlotte Brontë', *Essays and Studies by Members of the English Association*, 14 (1929) pp. 54–70.

Spielmann, M. H., *The Inner History of the Brontë–Heger Letters* (London,

1919).

Stevens, J. (ed.), *Mary Taylor, Friend of Charlotte Brontë: Letters from New Zealand and Elsewhere* (Oxford, 1972).

Stevenson, W. E., *Anne and Emily Brontë*, Profiles in Literature (London, 1968).

Sugden, K. A. R., *A Short History of the Brontës* (Oxford, 1929).

Tennyson, Sir C., *Alfred Tennyson* (London, 1850).

Tillotson, K., *Novels of the Eighteen-Forties* (Oxford, 1954).

Tompkins, J. M. S., 'Caroline Helstone's Eyes', *Brontë Society Transactions*, 71 (1961) pp. 18–28.

——, 'Jane Eyre's "Iron Shroud"', *Modern Language Review*, 22 (1927) pp. 195–7.

Tromley, A., *The Cover of the Mask: The Autobiographers in Charlotte Brontë's Fiction* (Victoria, 1982).

Weir, E., 'Cowan Bridge: New Light from Old Documents', *Brontë Society Transactions*, 56 (1946) pp. 16–28.

Wills, I. C., *The Authorship of Wuthering Heights* (London, 1936).

——, *The Brontës* (London, 1933).

Winnifrith, Tom, *The Brontës and their Background* (London, 1973).

——, *The Brontës* (London, 1977).

Woolf, V., '*Jane Eyre* and *Wuthering Heights*', in *The Common Reader*, first series (London, 1925) pp. 196–205.

Wroot, H. E., *The Persons and Places in the Brontë Novels* (Shipley, 1935).

Index